THE ULTIMATE BRAIN GAMES AND PUZZLES BOOK FOR ADULTS

Tricky But Fun Brain Teasers, Trivia Challenges, Crosswords, Word Searches And Much More To Keep Your Mind Young And Engaged

Donovan Ellis

CONTENTS

INTRODUCTION

Welcome to *The Ultimate Brain Games and Puzzles Book for Adults!*

Inside here are 150 puzzles, trivia quizzes, and fiendish word games to test your brainpower.

The puzzles are arranged in five sections, from easiest to hardest.

The first section is a warm-up area that just introduces some of the puzzles you'll find inside and explains how to play them (along with a few useful tactics you might need to solve them!).

Then there's an **EASY** section to get you started; a **MEDIUM** section that poses a little more of a challenge; a **HARD** section that will really begin test your brainpower; and a final **EXPERT** section that will take that challenge to the limit!

Don't worry if you get stuck or can't figure out an answer—all the solutions are at the back of the book, in simple numerical order.

Look out for some bonus trivia and **DID YOU KNOW's** along the way, but above all else—enjoy!

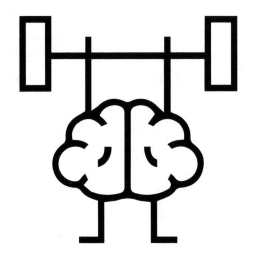

WARM-UP AREA

Take a few minutes to try out these practice puzzles.

These will explain how to play all the main puzzles and brain games
you'll find inside your *Ultimate Brain Games and Puzzles Book*.

PRACTISE SECTION 1
CROSSWORD

There are dozens of different crosswords inside *The Ultimate Brain Games and Puzzles Book*, from straightforward clue-solving games to mini games, anagram puzzles, and general knowledge quizzes.

Solve them all in the usual way: the clues are divided into Across and Down, and are numbered in order throughout the grid. Fill in the answers to the clues, letter by letter, into the grid, starting from the corresponding numbered square. Across answers read horizontally; Down answers read vertically.

Any overlapping words will share the same letter in the connecting square.

Try this quick puzzle to get started!

Across

1. One thing swapped for another (11)

7. Images taken with a camera (11)

8. Food stirrers (6)

9. Male offspring (pl.) (4)

11. Alongside, accompanying (4)

12. Not comfortable, on edge (6)

15. Mathematical chance (11)

16. Opposite of ancestors (11)

Down

1. Thick, tough cords (5)

2. Relative sizes (11)

3. Quantity (6)

4. Make money (4)

5. Discovering new territory (11)

6. Jobs, errands (5)

10. Longed for jealously (6)

11. Cleaned a surface (5)

13. Spinning toys on strings (2-3)

14. Female horse (4)

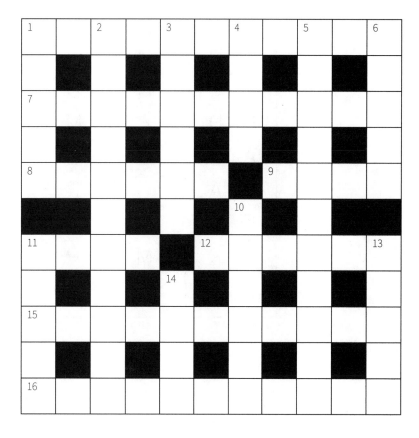

PRACTISE SECTION 2
Wordsearch

Find the listed clue words in the grid of jumbled letters. They can appear in any direction—forwards or backwards, upwards or downwards, horizontally, vertically, and diagonally.

Watch out for some of the trickier puzzles in the later pages—some of them have bonus games in which you might have to find extra words, decipher hidden phrases, or find words that aren't quite in the right order!

Some of the clue words are split up, so you'll have to find ALL their individual parts in the grid. If a clue word were listed as "WORD / SEARCH", for instance, you would have to find both WORD and SEARCH in the puzzle as separate answers.

Here's a quick mini game to get you started—find all 20 of these girls' names in the grid below.

```
A  J  K  B  A  R  B  A  R  A
N  A  N  I  C  O  L  E  I  N
D  N  R  U  T  H  D  R  P  N
R  E  A  H  T  D  A  A  F  E
E  D  C  E  I  M  I  A  W  Y
A  L  H  L  I  L  Y  A  P  N
Y  A  E  E  U  R  D  P  N  M
E  U  L  N  A  C  O  A  W  A
V  R  N  M  M  P  Y  F  G  U
E  A  M  E  L  I  A  G  U  D
```

Amelia	Diana	Laura	Maud
Andrea	Eve	Lily	Nicole
Anne	Helen	Lucy	Poppy
Barbara	Hilda	Maria	Rachel
Dawn	Jane	Mary	Ruth

PRACTISE SECTION 3
ACROSTIC

In an acrostic puzzle, the answers to all 20 clues are the same length.

Fill them into the grid in numerical order, from top to bottom, into the corresponding rows. Some of the letters will be filled in already to help you make a start.

Once all the answers are written in the grid, a hidden phrase will be spelled out by the first letters of each word in order, reading top to bottom in the shaded column. It could be a saying, the title of a book, a place, a movie, a sporting event—anything at all! Find this hidden phrase to complete the puzzle.

Try this shorter 10-word game to get used to how to play.

1. Christmas month (8)

2. The ABCs (8)

3. Opposite of horizontal (8)

4. Frozen dairy dessert (8)

5. Flying __, legendary ghost ship (8)

6. New York's nickname (8)

7. Someone who always looks on the bright side (8)

8. American artist, known for his portrait of his mother (8)

9. Said a rude remark to (8)

10. It's presented as proof in court (8)

#							
1					B		
2		P					
3					C		
4			C				M
5	U			H			
6					P		
7	P						
8			S				
9			U				
10	V					C	

ⓘ DID YOU KNOW?

The artist mentioned in CLUE 8 here was born in Lowell, Massachusetts, in 1834 – though he later disowned his hometown, and severed any connection to it. "I shall be born when and where I want," he declared, "and I do not choose to be born in Lowell!"

A codeword is a crossword with no clues! All the letters have been replaced with numbers—so A could be 1, B could be 2, and so on. All you have to do is figure out which number corresponds to which letter.

You'll be given three letters in the correct places to get started, so right away you can go ahead and fill in all the numbers in the grid matching theirs. Then, based on how they fall into place, see how many of the other letters and words you can figure out and take it from there!

Use the alphabet and the reference grid below the main one to keep track of which numbers and letters you've solved so far, and which are still left to work out.

Here's a quick game to have a go at first. P, I, and A are already in the grid, at the end of a five—letter word. You can go ahead and fill in all the other Ps, Is, and As based on their numbers here. After that, what five—letter word might that be on the third row? Something to do with old photographs perhaps…?

	3		16		25	9	7	18	2
10	2	23	13	18			13		10
	20		6		8	25	21 P	1 I	2 A
17	25	15	26		13		8		14
11		13		2	6	26	2	6	1
2	5	5	13	18	12		1		17
17		5		1		4	6	13	24
15	18	25	25	12		2		21	
25		25			21	1	19	11	25
8	11	8	22	1		7		8	

A B C D E F G H I J K L M N O P Q R S T U V W X Y Z

1	2	3	4	5	6	7	8	9	10	11	12	13
14	15	16	17	18	19	20	21	22	23	24	25	26

PRACTISE SECTION 5
Pop Quiz

Test your general knowledge with a pop quiz! There are dozens of trivia quizzes scattered throughout the book, with questions covering everything from sport and science to music and math.

Keep an eye out for some of the quizzes that have a little bit of a twist—some of the games will have a theme; some will have a secret connection between all their answers; and in some you'll have to come up with two answers to score a point!

To get warmed up, here's an easier round to get you started. All the answers to these questions begin with the letter M... See how many points you can score out of a maximum of 15!

1. What is the most populous city in Wisconsin?
2. Who was Lennon's famous songwriting partner?
3. In what game can you go to jail, win a beauty contest, and mortgage a train station?
4. What can be handlebar, pencil, walrus, and Dali?
5. Who is the author of the first book of the *New Testament*?
6. Which queen of England was known for her "bloody" reputation?
7. Glacier National Park is found in which of the US states?
8. Which country band had a worldwide hit with "Dance the Night Away" in 1998?
9. What Stephen King story is about a novelist trapped in a deranged fan's isolated home?
10. What were First Ladies Washington and Jefferson both called?
11. What vegetarian marine mammal is also known as the sea cow?
12. Mazatlán is a coastal city in what country?
13. What name is given to a follower of Islam?
14. What famous Hollywood star is known for the catchphrase, "Come up and see me sometime"?
15. What musical stage show and movie is based on the songs by the pop group ABBA?
16. Sicily and Malta are islands in what sea?
17. What animated character who debuted in 1949 is known for his comically bad eyesight?
18. What famous make of German automobile has a three-pronged star as its logo?
19. What is Orlando's NBA team called?
20. What 1851 novel opens with the line, "Call me Ishmael"?

---

❶ *DID YOU KNOW?*

In 1992, ABBA singer Anni-Frid Lyngstad married into the royal family of Europe's ancient House of Reuss - so her proper title is now Princess Anni-Frid of Reuss, Dowager Countess of Plauen.

PRACTISE SECTION 6
Brainteasers

Alongside all the classic puzzles on offer here, there are lots of mini games too. The rules of each one will be explained as we go along, but here are a few to give you an idea of what to expect. First of all, what word fits this hangman-style template?

SP __ __ __ G __ __ ME

PRACTISE SECTION 7
Pyramids

This is a word pyramid. Each answer contains all the letters of the previous one jumbled up, plus one new letter. Can you fill in all eight remaining rows to complete the grid?

1. Like, similar to (2)

2. Ocean (3)

3. Cook meat quickly in intense heat (4)

4. Delete, get rid of (5)

5. Springtime Christian festival (6)

6. Severe, harsh, and unfeeling (7)

7. It's found where X marks the spot (8)

8. Animals (9)

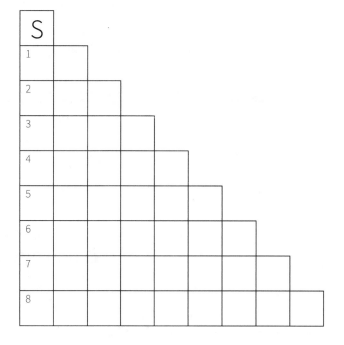

PRACTISE SECTION 8
MULTIJUMBLES

This is a multijumble! THREE Canadian provinces have had their names jumbled together here, and their letters placed in alphabetical order. Can you unpick them and put them back in the corresponding boxes? Some of the letters have been filled in to help you make a start.

~~A~~ ~~A~~ A A ~~B~~ B C ~~E~~ E E H K L N Q R S S T T U W

				E			B			

	A		A						

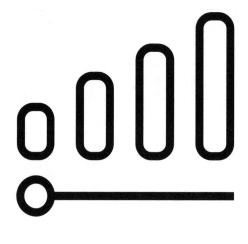

EASY

Now you're familiar with the rules, let's get things started.

This first section keeps things a little easier…

9

Across

7. Melt away (8)

9. Seats (6)

10. Notion (4)

11. Unmoving (10)

12. Area (6)

14. Set free (8)

15. Music for a singer (13)

17. Menace, intimidate (8)

19. Refuses to allow (6)

21. Printed journals (10)

22. Finishes (4)

23. Send a message (6)

24. As a baby starting to bite (8)

Down

1. Violin (6)

2. Largest continent (4)

3. Metal used to make kitchen foil (8)

4. Educational establishment (6)

5. A national political body (10)

6. Search for gold (8)

8. Amusement (13)

13. Growing, enlarging (10)

15. Sporty (8)

16. Put money into a business (8)

18. Paths (6)

20. Conclusion to a film or story (6)

22. Reverberating noise (4)

ⓘ DID YOU KNOW?

The world's largest continent—the answer to 2 DOWN—is also the world's most populous. It covers almost 10% of the entire surface of the Earth; occupies 30% of all the land surface; and is home to 60% of all the people!

10

See if you can find all these lakes, seas, and oceans in the grid below.

Adriatic
Aral Sea
Atlantic
Baffin Bay
Baikal
Balkash
Baltic
Bass Sea
Bering Sea
Black Sea
Caribbean
Coral Sea
Hudson Bay
Irish Sea
Kara Sea
Lake Chad
Lake Ladoga
Loch Ness
North Sea
Pacific
Red Sea

```
H C O R A L S E A K
X N N N A B R D R L
U B I K N A E A I A
B L I A O L D D P K
Q A F R R K S R A E
B C S A T A E I C C
A K D S H S A A I H
T S G E S H Q T F A
L E Q A E E L I I D
A A Y I A A A C C T
N G D U B V I O D I
T L O C H N E S S R
I A R A L S E A L I
C A R I B B E A N S
H U D S O N B A Y H
B A F F I N B A Y S
B E R I N G S E A E
L A K E L A D O G A
```

ⓘ *DID YOU KNOW?*

Lake Balkash in eastern Kazakhstan, listed here, is one of the largest lakes in the world. It is split into two halves, east and west, divided by a narrow strait—but while the eastern side of the lake is salty, the western half is freshwater.

11

Across

1. Theatrical work (5)

4. Rigid (5)

5. A wizard's incantation (5)

Down

1. School tables (5)

2. Similar (5)

3. Horrible (5)

12

1. Pennsylvania

2. Snake said to have killed Cleopatra

3. Discomfort

4. Country between France and Portugal

5. Painful contortion of a joint

6. Old term for someone from Iran

7. Artists who use brushes

8. Shelled water-dwelling reptiles

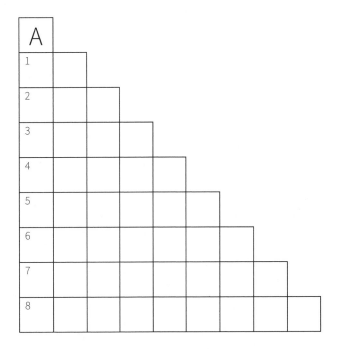

ⓘ DID YOU KNOW?

The famous story of Cleopatra committing suicide by snakebite—CLUE 2 here—is perhaps only a legend. The Roman historian Plutarch later wrote that "what really took place is known to no one," and admitted Cleopatra's death remains a mystery.

13

1. Moby-Dick author Herman (8)

2. Questionable (8)

3. Surgical cut (8)

4. Eleventh month (8)

5. Three-sided shape (8)

6. Obvious (8)

7. Created (8)

8. Rough pad of paper (8)

9. Unlucky number (8)

10. Luckless, unlikely to succeed (8)

11. Raised, lifted (8)

12. Outgoings; exchanging cash (8)

13. The day after today (8)

14. Suddenly, without warning (8)

15. Agricultural vehicles (8)

16. Rain shade (8)

17. Cutting tool (8)

18. Arguments (8)

19. On the floor above (8)

20. Points of view (8)

1						L
2		G				
3		C				
4						
5						
6			A			
7						
8					O	
9						
10		P				
11			V			
12				D		
13						
14				P		
15						
16						
17			S	S		
18						
19	P					
20					O	

ⓘ DID YOU KNOW?

Despite its popularity today Moby-Dick, —CLUE 1 here—was originally something of a failure, and sold fewer than 4,000 copies during its author's lifetime.

9	15	7	4	7		4	5	13	4	20	26	15	14	2
19		24		25		25		14		9		8		4
23 Y	14 O	22 U		6	25	9		8	4	4	26	15	2	10
8		4		4		2		21		7		26		12
4	1	4	2		17	4	12	15	21	4	9	25	26	4
		16		15		7		2		2		26		13
7	19	4	12	12		26	9	4	25	26	8	4	2	26
4				12					15				4
13	14	8	20	22	26	4	9	7		2	25	18	4	17
14		15		7		12		25		10		2		
2	15	2	4	26	4	4	2	26	19		3	14	21	7
17		22		9		13		15		16		11		26
25	26	26	9	25	13	26		7	19	4		15	13	4
9		4		26		4		6		9		2		9
23	4	7	26	4	9	17	25	23		14	9	10	25	2

A B C D E F G H I J K L M N O P Q R S T U V W X Y Z

1	2	3	4	5	6	7	8	9	10	11	12	13
14	15	16	17	18	19	20	21	22	23	24	25	26

🛈 DID YOU KNOW?

In English, referring to someone as "you" was once seen as polite or respectful; if you were talking to someone you knew well, it was more normal to say "thou".

15

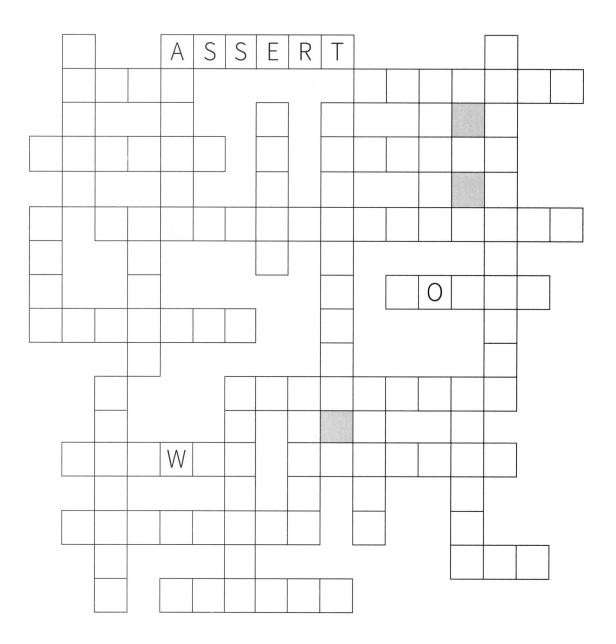

3 letters
Yak

4 letters
Read
Tell

5 letters
Opine
Orate
Reply

Spiel
State
Utter
Voice

6 letters
Affirm
Allege
Answer
Assert
Convey

Remark
Render

7 letters
Declare
Imagine
Mention
Perform
Respond

8 letters
Disclose

9 letters
Make known
Pronounce

11 letters
Communicate

15 letters
Break the silence

16

There are 26 questions in this pop quiz—one for every letter of the alphabet. The answer to each question begins with a different letter from A to Z; no letter is used more than once.

A B C D E F G H I J K L M N O P Q R S T U V W X Y Z

1. Hokkaido is northernmost of the four main islands of which country?

2. What musical instrument can be snare, kettle, or bass?

3. What rock group had 90s hits with "Everybody Hurts" and "Shiny Happy People"?

4. What was the first name of the Hungarian socialite and actress Gabor who died in 2016?

5. The patella is the bone forming what joint in the body?

6. What creatures live in social groups called prides?

7. What grayish metal was once made of tin mixed with lead, but now contains antimony?

8. What US state has a coast on Puget Sound?

9. What type of building was originally defined in the late 1800s as any building having more than 10 stories?

10. What is meat from an adult sheep commonly known as…?

11. …and what is meat from a deer known as?

12. What are there 36 of in a yard?

13. What novel by JRR Tolkien features a dragon named Smaug?

14. In what country were Celine Dion, Alanis Morissette, k.d. lang, and Neil Young all born?

15. In what month is St. Valentine's Day?

16. Named after a city in the southeast of France, what name is given to a salad of tomatoes, olives, hard-boiled eggs, and either anchovies or tuna?

17. How are members of the Religious Society of Friends better known?

18. What Spanish city hosted the 1992 Olympic Games?

19. Who is the Norwegian composer of In the "Hall of the Mountain King"?

20. What African nation was once ruled by Idi Amin?

21. How many instruments are there in an octet?

22. In the world of superhero movies, what are Wolverine, Cyclops, and Beast?

23. What word would come next after ultimate, and penultimate?

24. What video sharing website has a red and white play button as its logo?

25. What would you find at the junction of Broadway, Seventh Avenue, and 42nd Street?

26. What stage musical features the songs "Food Glorious Food" and "As Long as He Needs Me"?

17

Across

6. A flat area of high ground (7)

7. Brings into effect, uses (7)

9. Extremely angry (5)

10. Waited a moment (9)

11. Not as long (7)

13. Measure of temperature (6)

15. It's abbreviated to "ad" (13)

19. Grunted like a pig (6)

20. Allowed, let pass (7)

23. Southeast's opposite (9)

24. A sill beneath a window (5)

26. Absolute quiet (7)

27. In opposition to (7)

Down

1. Molten rock (4)

2. Turn down (6)

3. Power, influence (9)

4. On a river, further from the coast (8)

5. They're left by walkers on sand or mud (10)

6. Cleric (6)

7. Household powdery dirt (4)

8. Unanticipated (6)

12. Normally (10)

14. Absolutely necessary (9)

16. Gigantic tusked mammal (8)

17. Elbows and knees, for example (6)

18. Most peculiar (6)

21. Basement (6)

22. Used to be (4)

25. Refuse to allow (4)

18

Eleven classic Marylin Monroe movies are listed in the grid.

```
G A M I L L I O N A I R E N D
E T H T O K N O C K T H R F Q
N H O H N I A G A R A U S V U
T E W E Z Y E A R I T C H K O
L M T A R B X T D E U R C W T
E I O S I L T O R G E W D Q H
M S M P V O T O V F N P E J E
E F A H E N N H E D O L F F S
N I R A R D V R E T B F I B H
F T R L O E P K S S D U U O O
Y S Y T F S D S I Z E V N I W
J U N G L E U U Y H H V O S G
S D O N T B O T H E R N E S I
T H E P R I N C E A N D G N R
Y S O M E L I K E I T H O T L
```

Bus Stop

Don't Bother / To Knock

Gentlemen / Prefer / Blondes

How to Marry / A Millionaire

Niagara

River of / No Return

Some Like it Hot

The Asphalt / Jungle

The Misfits

The Prince and / the Showgirl

The Seven / Year Itch

ℹ️ DID YOU KNOW?

Marylin's name was famously a stage name; her real name was Norma Jean Baker. But "Marylin Monroe" wasn't Norma's first choice—if she had gone with her initial choice of stage name, she would have been known forever as Jean Adair.

19

Across

1. Hurt by a bee (5)

4. Black and white African mammal (5)

5. Performs a song (5)

Down

1. Small, medium, or large (5)

2. In the city (5)

3. Cogs (5)

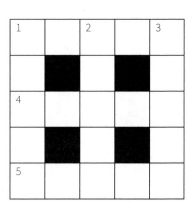

20

What word is this?

_ _ _ **KC** _ **S** _

21

1. Pertaining to (abbrev.) (2)

2. Long period of time (3)

3. Challenge (4)

4. Reviewed, gave a score (5)

5. Fabric cord (6)

6. Width (7)

7. Inhaled and exhaled (8)

8. Chattered nonsensically (9)

22

1. Tired, exhausted (4-3)

2. Animal's environment (7)

3. Natural wearing away (7)

4. More agile (7)

5. Sore (7)

6. Most unsightly (7)

7. Shrieks (7)

8. Fit (7)

9. Orange root vegetables (7)

10. Plantation of fruit trees (7)

11. Gigantic (7)

12. Simplest (7)

13. Screenplays (7)

14. Congested vehicles (7)

15. Not indoors (7)

16. Talented (7)

17. Major German city (7)

18. Large flightless bird (7)

19. Gap for a new employee (7)

20. Attracted, lured (7)

#						
1				O		
2		B				
3		O				
4			B			
5						
6	G					
7						
8					H	
9						
10			H			
11						E
12						
13				P		
14						C
15						
16						D
17		M				
18						
19						Y
20				C		

ⓘ DID YOU KNOW?

The Latin name for the large flightless bird named in CLUE 18 is "Struthio"—which despite the bird's enormous size, derives from the Greek word for a sparrow!

23

	11	13	3	24	15	2		13	20	12	9	24	15	
11		16		20		5		3		9		12		8
26	16	20	25	22	12	15		16	15	7	25	9	16	15
20		22		1		2		19		25		4		3
16	15	12	9	15	17		3		12	9	14 Z	3 A	16 R	2
15		15		22	12	20	24	19	15	2		26		15
2	3	4	13		3		8		26		16	15	3	2
				26	11	8	9	16	26	11				
8	9	13	11		8		15		25		13	15	15	12
9		25		11	15	16	21	9	24	15		6		3
10	25	4	13	15	2		15		15	6	13	15	24	26
3		13		21		17		11		13		24		15
24	8	9	18	15	11	15		13	15	3	18	25	26	11
19		18		16		15		25		18		26		26
	3	23	16	15	15	2		18	20	2	2	15	2	

A B C D E F G H I J K L M N O P Q R S T U V W X Y Z

1	2	3	4	5	6	7	8	9	10	11	12	13
14	15	16	17	18	19	20	21	22	23	24	25	26

❶ DID YOU KNOW?

The word that's partly in the grid above is the name of an animal—the largest of which is native to just one island in Indonesia, and grows to more than 10ft in length.

24

What word is this?

FOO __ __ __ OOF

25

The names of THREE famous movie directors have been jumbled up here, and the letters placed in alphabetical order. Unpick them and put them back in the corresponding boxes.

A A B C C C E E G H̶ H I I I K L̶ N N O̶ O̶ P R R S T T T

| | | | | H | | O | | | | P | | L | | | |

| | | | | | | | O | |

26

A wordsearch with a twist! The names of 14 creepy-crawlies have been jumbled up. Solve their anagrams, then search for their names in the grid.

At kiddy
Awe rig
Bald guy
Deck bar
Emitter
Leaf
Lye riff
Ousel
Prides
Rec tick
Tan
Tang
Throne
Tom gag

T	E	R	M	I	T	E	L	J	O
G	A	N	T	I	L	O	U	S	E
K	I	N	G	T	E	N	R	O	H
K	P	W	G	U	D	S	S	N	F
A	M	A	R	E	B	P	J	H	I
T	A	A	B	A	I	Y	I	T	R
Y	G	U	T	D	E	Y	D	Y	E
D	G	A	E	A	E	L	F	A	F
I	O	R	E	D	B	A	C	K	L
D	T	E	K	C	I	R	C	W	Y

18	2	15	19	■	13 (A)	14 (C)	17 (H)	21	4
2	■	7	■	12	■	17	■	24	■
13	4	4	15	23	15	8	7	13	9
16	■	15	■	8	■	19	■	15	■
23	■	1	15	26	21	■	13	9	21
6	8	8	■	21	26	15	9	■	25
■	25	■	12	■	21	■	20	■	15
11	15	23	23	21	16	20	2	1	12
■	4	■	22	■	22	■	24	■	23
10	21	3	21	16	■	13	12	5	12

A B C D E F G H I J K L M N O P Q R S T U V W X Y Z

1	2	3	4	5	6	7	8	9	10	11	12	13
14	15	16	17	18	19	20	21	22	23	24	25	26

28

The first nine answers here are all connected. Work out that connection for a bonus tenth point!

1. In the famous poem, which animals go to sea "in a beautiful pea-green boat"?

2. Which rock group's hits include "Hotel California" and "Lyin' Eyes"?

3. What novel by Dashiell Hammett was made into a 1941 Humphrey Bogart movie?

4. What senior member of the Catholic Church is ranked immediately behind the pope?

5. What are the local Major League Baseball team based in Toronto called?

6. What is the common name for the highly contagious childhood disease, varicella?

7. What Tchaikovsky ballet was originally a failure when it premiered in 1877?

8. What collection of children's horror stories was written by RL Stine?

9. Who voiced the Genie in Disney's *Aladdin*?

10. What connects all nine of these answers?

29

Across

8. Amaze (4)

9. Eatery (10)

10. Clothing, getup (6)

11. Laterally (8)

12. Mix (4)

13. The gases around the Earth (10)

17. Makes mistakes (4)

18. Slim-fitting (5)

19. Tube, conduit (4)

20. Plug-in (10)

22. A musical tone (4)

23. Ambushed (8)

27. Tiny (6)

28. TV (10)

29. A dolt (4)

Down

1. Architectural (10)

2. Formal school clothes (8)

3. An instrument for measuring angles (10)

4. Utilizes (4)

5. Stiff paper; a greeting mailed on a birthday (4)

6. Enlargement (6)

7. Solely (4)

14. Sorcery (5)

15. A legal deal (10)

16. Renown (10)

19. A pocket blade (8)

21. Ran after (6)

24. Digits of the feet (4)

25. Make fabric with yarn (4)

26. Droplet of liquid (4)

30

```
B R I N G T O A H E A D R M L
E T T U B R U T E N N A G U T
I Q N H D Y U E I I E N O M F
I H F B T O M E H N I S F S H
O H Z N M S Y C A H D C F T P
I M B D I E S D S N C A Y H A
S U U E Y S N A A E H P O E R
F O O M A E B Y Q S I I U W M
L W T L L R D Y C G N N R O I
T O G T A O A D G K W H H R N
G Y Y E B K M R L B A A E D A
M Q N V Z U W D M O G N A B R
F A N C Y F R E E S T D D X M
F R O G I N T H E T H R O A T
P U T Y O U R F O O T D O W N
```

Arm in arm

Bear arms

Body and soul

Bring to a head

Cap in hand

Chin wag

Et tu, brute?

Fancy free

Frog in the throat

Glass chin

Got my eye in

Lend an ear

Loudmouth

Mum's the word

Off your head

Put your foot down

Woe is me!

ℹ️ DID YOU KNOW?

Julius Caesar's famous last word's, "Et tu, Brute?"—literally "You too, Brutus?"—are actually just his last lines in William Shakespeare's famous play, Julius Caesar. According to the Roman historian Suetonius, Caesar's last words were actually "You too, child?", and were spoken in Greek—"Kai su, teknon?" According to Plutarch, meanwhile, Caesar said nothing at all!

31

Across

1. Threaded fastener (5)

4. Sacked (5)

5. Ran a country (5)

Down

1. Less dangerous (5)

2. In the countryside (5)

3. Trudged through water (5)

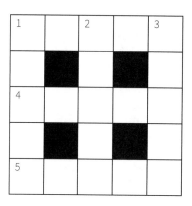

32

1. Georgia (2)

2. Tattered fabric (3)

3. Anger (4)

4. Level; student's mark (5)

5. Black and white animal that lives in a sett (6)

6. Cut short a text (7)

7. Divisions of an army (8)

8. Aviaries (9)

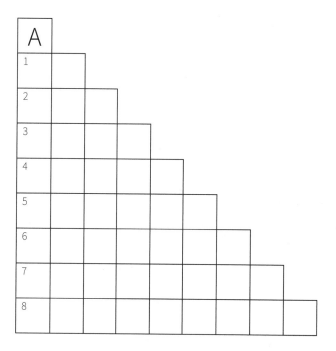

ⓘ DID YOU KNOW?

The state of Georgia has had five capitals: Savannah (1777–85), Augusta (1786–89), Louisville (1789-1807), Milledgeville (1807–67), and now Atlanta (since 1868).

33

1. The Oilers' and the Bruins' sports (3,6)

2. Massachusetts island (9)

3. Black and white spotty dog (9)

4. Undone, like a belt or shoe (9)

5. Occasionally (9)

6. Thus (9)

7. Re-educated, retaught (9)

8. Cleverness, wits (9)

9. A describing word (9)

10. Places (9)

11. Replied (9)

12. All people (9)

13. Almost, practically (9)

14. Surgical procedure (9)

15. Legal get-outs (9)

16. Unaltered (9)

17. PT, MT, CT, and ET, for example (4,5)

18. Butt in (9)

19. Medical salves (9)

20. Of an animal: active at night (9)

---

❶ DID YOU KNOW?

According to legend, the Massachusetts island that is the answer to CLUE 2 here was purchased for the sum of "30 pounds and two beaver-pelt hats" by European Governor Thomas Mayhew. Through his daughter Martha (b.1642), he is a distant relative of the pop superstar Taylor Swift.

1								
2						K		
3		L						
4					K			
5								S
6					F			
7		T						D
8				L	L			
9		J						
10		C						
11						D		
12	V							
13				U				
14								
15				H				
16		C						
17								
18						U		
19	I							
20								

A B C D E F G H I J K L M N O P Q R S T U V W X Y Z

1	2	3	4	5	6	7	8	9	10	11	12	13
14	15	16	17	18	19	20	21	22	23	24	25	26

35

What word is this?

__ R __ F __ __ S __ __ N __ __

36

Can you find all the traditional Chinese zodiac animals in the grid?

Buffalo   Pig

Dog   Rabbit

Dragon   Rat

Goat   Rooster

Horse   Snake

Monkey   Tiger

B	D	O	G	V	L	Z	R
R	U	R	H	O	D	R	O
A	M	F	A	O	A	A	O
B	W	O	F	G	R	T	S
B	C	L	N	A	O	S	T
I	S	G	W	K	L	N	E
T	I	G	E	R	E	O	R
P	S	N	A	K	E	Y	G

37

This is an anagram acrostic—reshuffle the clue words and put them into the right places in the grid to spell out a hidden word reading downwards in the shaded column.

1. Freight   **6.** Baldies

2. Tsarina   **7.** Abactor

3. Demures   **8.** Brawler

4. Amenity   **9.** Anodyne

5. Engined   **10.** Deedily

#						
1		G				
2						N
3			U			
4		Y				
5						G
6				B		
7	C					
8			B			
9				Y		
10						D

38

All the answers to these questions have the same two initials. Can you work out what they are?

1. In what 1986 movie did Tom Cruise play US Navy pilot Pete Maverick?

2. What part of the eye contains a series of tubes called lacrimal ducts?

3. The Caribbean nation of St Vincent is paired with what island group, including the islands of Mustique and Bequia?

4. What Mario Puzo novel was adapted for the cinema in 1972?

5. What is driving behind another vehicle without leaving sufficient distance called?

6. Which Monty Python member directed *Fear and Loathing in Las Vegas*?

7. What fashion outlet was founded in San Francisco in 1969?

8. What 1969 movie features Rooster Cogburn?

9. Which English poet composed the famous poem, "Elegy Written in a Country Churchyard"?

10. Banjul is the capital of what West African nation?

…And now the answers to these questions have those initials in reverse order…

11. What does a left point arrow (>) mean in math?

12. Who played Lieutenant Sulu in the original Star Trek series?

13. What "Harlem" exhibition basketball team were founded in 1926?

14. What is German for "good day"?

15. What is an abandoned settlement typically known as?

16. Where in London were many of Shakespeare's plays first performed?

17. What 1970s sitcom starring Esther Rolle and John Amos was a spinoff from *Maude*?

18. What item of sports equipment is typically made of wood or plastic, and stands 2 1/8"?

19. What 1726 novel is set in fictional places called Lilliput and Brobdingnag?

20. Which American actress played the title role in 1944's *Laura*?

---

❶ DID YOU KNOW?

Bea Arthur's hit sitcom Maude was itself a spinoff from Carroll O'Connor's All in the Family—which makes the answer to this question the first spinoff from a spinoff in American television history!

MEDIUM

Let's make things a little trickier…

39

Across

8. Of a wound: raw (6)

9. Dependable (8)

10. Vessel (4)

11. In all places (10)

12. Unspoiled (4)

13. Extraordinary (10)

17. Footwear (4)

18. Exams (5)

19. Closed (4)

21. Of the past (10)

23. Theatrical performers of a play (4)

24. Distasteful (10)

28. Curved structure (4)

29. A living thing (8)

30. In a single direction (3-3)

Down

1. However (8)

2. A perfect accompaniment (10)

3. Machine for producing text (10)

4. Genuine (4)

5. Cohort, friend (4)

6. Clean with water (4)

7. Not singular (6)

14. Melodic sound (5)

15. New Year promise (10)

16. Related, linked together (10)

20. Not fond of other people (8)

22. Pay no notice to (6)

25. Tilt (4)

26. Extremely dry (4)

27. Military force (4)

40

All the countries and nations—past and present—listed in the grid have seven letters.

```
G E R M A N Y E B R I T A I N
I R E L A N D Y B U R U N D I
A I U G B O R X M Y A N M A R
R T R R R A R N V A N U A T U
M R U E G G M O L D O V A U L
E E G N L E B A N O N A R N K
N A U A E O R A L F I U Y I M
I H A D J R L X D G G S A S O
A O Y A O G U B O S E T N I R
A U S D N I P A T O R R T A O
S E N E G A L H P M I I I Y C
Z A D E N M A R K A A A G A C
D A H O M E Y A B L Y G U Z O
C R O A T I A I F I N L A N D
B E L G I U M N J A M A I C A
```

Antigua	Burundi	Georgia	Lebanon	Senegal
Armenia	Croatia	Germany	Moldova	Somalia
Austria	Denmark	Grenada	Morocco	Tunisia
Bahrain	England	Hungary	Myanmar	Uruguay
Belgium	Eritrea	Ireland	Nigeria	Vanuatu
Britain	Finland	Jamaica		

---

❶ DID YOU KNOW?

At just over 130 sq miles, Grenada is the smallest country on this list. The island was once privately owned, but in 1664 the French king Louis XIV bought the island from a count in his court, and operated it as part of his French West India trade company. When the company dissolved a decade later it became a French crown colony, and later a nation in its own right!

41

This is just like a standard crossword, but with a twist: all the answers are anagrams of the clue words. Can you unscramble the clues to complete the grid?

Across

1. Aimed (5)

4. Lamp (4)

7. Reductions (10)

8. Censer (6)

10. Rested (6)

15. Resectable (10)

16. Op-ed (4)

17. Sayer (5)

Down

1. Limas (5)

2. Treed (5)

3. Donate (6)

5. Char (4)

6. Sham (4)

9. Barney (6)

11. Taxer (5)

12. Setts (5)

13. Dice (4)

14. Lops (4)

42

1. "Keep quiet!" (2)

2. Remnant of a fire (3)

3. Hurry; a stroke or hyphen (4)

4. Shadow (5)

5. Split equally (6)

6. Toughest, most solid (7)

7. Upper cushion of a driver's seat (8)

8. Smashed or broken to pieces (9)

43

1. October 31

2. Rude, unpleasant

3. Thunderbolt

4. Without end, infinite

5. Day before today

6. Holder for a decorative display of flowers on the side of a house (6,3)

7. Else, in which case

8. Furthest from the midpoint

9. The body's processing of food

10. Eligible males

11. Enormous unit of astronomical distance (5,4)

12. Trinkets

13. Tough, thick paper used to make boxes

14. What is known

15. Fundamentally

16. Clothes beneath clothes

17. Most peculiar

18. Provisional; short-lasting

19. Moving staircase

20. Oblong

	1	2	3	4	5	6	7	8	9
1									
2		F					I		
3			G						
4						L			
5									Y
6						W			X
7			H						E
8		U				M			
9			G						
10			C						
11						Y	E		
12		R							
13					B				
14				W					E
15					C				
16			D						
17									
18				P			A		
19		S							
20									

❶ DID YOU KNOW?

The unit of distance that is the answer to CLUE 11 is equal to 5.88 trillion miles!

7	26	20	20	13	24	24	19	19	■	25	1	19	21	25
23	■	19	■	14	■	13	■	5	■	13	■	5	■	8
21	22	21	1	25	19	25	■	6	19	21	7	3	19	4
4	■	4	■	13	■	15	■	1	■	12	■	13	■	24
4 (S)	11	8	19	21	17	■	24	19	1	1	13	2	23	15
1 (R)	■	1	■	14	■	6	■	4	■	21	■	13	■	■
26 (O)	10	19	14	■	7	23	21	4	4	20	21	24	19	4
26	■	■	■	7	■	21	■	13	■	4	■	■	■	19
20	21	12	14	13	18	15	13	14	12	■	17	19	19	6
■	■	21	■	24	■	12	■	12	■	3	■	14	■	21
22	21	1	1	13	26	1	4	■	22	21	14	25	19	1
13	■	2	■	16	■	26	■	9	■	22	■	13	■	21
6	23	21	24	19	21	8	■	21	12	21	13	14	4	24
19	■	12	■	14	■	14	■	22	■	13	■	12	■	19
4	24	19	20	4	■	25	13	4	20	13	4	4	19	25

A B C D E F G H I J K L M N O P Q R S T U V W X Y Z

1	2	3	4	5	6	7	8	9	10	11	12	13
14	15	16	17	18	19	20	21	22	23	24	25	26

45

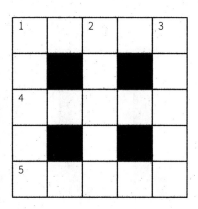

Across

1. Snapshot (5)

4. Ascend (5)

5. Pleasant smell (5)

Down

1. Fills luggage (5)

2. Salty grape-like fruit (5)

3. Circle around (5)

46

Blizzard
Cloud
Drift
Flood
Frost
Gales
Hail
Heatwave
Hurricane
Lightning
Rain
Snow
Sun
Thunder
Tornado
Wind

S	H	O	N	K	R	D	U	E	S
N	E	D	S	A	O	N	F	N	R
B	A	A	I	U	E	I	O	A	R
L	T	N	D	B	N	W	T	C	E
I	W	R	O	U	F	D	S	I	D
Z	A	O	O	C	R	E	O	R	N
Z	V	T	L	I	L	M	R	R	U
A	E	O	F	A	D	A	F	U	H
R	U	T	G	H	A	I	L	H	T
D	G	N	I	N	T	H	G	I	L

ⓘ DID YOU KNOW?

The US certain gets more than its fair share of tornadoes—but by area, the country that experiences the most tornadoes per square mile is actually the United Kingdom. Although storms in the UK are much less severe than in the US, on average the UK reports two tornadoes for every 10,000 sq km (3,800 sq miles) of its territory, which equates to one tornado per 1,750 sq miles. The US, by comparison, averages only one tornado every 2,900 sq miles.

47

	9		3		22	6	24	24	17
2	17	18	11	7	■	■	6	■	8
■	2	■	8	■	17 A	26 N	2 V	8	9
23	17	19	19	■	4	■	17	■	24
17	■	8	■	20	7	10	10	9	7
22	17	20	7	15	5	■	9	■	26
21	■	22	■	17	■	13	7	20	16
7	10	6	26	1	■	17	■	7	■
16	■	12	■	■	6	25	25	7	15
5	14	7	9	9	■	16	■	21	■

A B C D E F G H I J K L M N O P Q R S T U V W X Y Z

1	2	3	4	5	6	7	8	9	10	11	12	13
14	15	16	17	18	19	20	21	22	23	24	25	26

48

Another pop quiz with a twist. The answers to these nine questions have something in common. Work out the link between everything for a bonus tenth point!

1. "Fill the mead cup, drain the barrel" is a line from what traditional Christmas carol?

2. What movie, first released in 1933, was remade in 1976 and again in 2005?

3. What is an especially skilled and successful fighter pilot known as?

4. Brisbane is the capital of what Australian state?

5. What game is played on a ship by pushing weighted discs along the deck into a scoring zone?

6. What 2010s legal drama was Meghan Markle starring in when she met Prince Harry?

7. What is the hardest naturally occurring material on Earth?

8. What American actor won an Oscar for his role in *City Slickers*?

9. What part of the body is scanned in an electrocardiogram?

10. What is the connection between these answers?

49

Across

6. Whirlwind (7)

7. Suggest (7)

9. Punctuation mark (5)

10. Convinces (9)

11. More fortunate (7)

13. Mixed eggs (6)

15. Inspection (13)

19. Of the sea, rough and undulating (6)

20. An ambassador's residence (7)

23. Schoolroom (9)

24. Horrible (5)

26. Of a species: no longer living (7)

27. Saw, spotted (7)

Down

1. Cut shorter (4)

2. Island state (6)

3. Work together (9)

4. File (8)

5. Stipulations to a deal (10)

6. Touch lightly to make laugh (6)

7. Meat from a pig (4)

8. Making less hard, alleviating (6)

12. Opposite of vowels (10)

14. Concord, seeing eye to eye (9)

16. Revealing (8)

17. Frozen spike of water (6)

18. Biked (6)

21. Animals, wild creatures (6)

22. Coastal settlement (4)

25. Visage (4)

50

Thirteen Dickens novels are listed in this grid.

```
B A R N A B Y R U D G E K I T
D Y X C O P P E R F I E L D H
O O T W O C I T I E S G Y G E
M P R P A J P V I W W B K E P
B H K R W M O L I V E R S X I
E A N P I T H E O L D U L P C
Y R I A G T Y N K B O A I E K
A D C P R C H C A H U H T C W
N T H E E K I M K T D T T T I
D I O R A N B A U Q A T L A C
S M L S T K E M Q T S L E T K
O E A M Z L R M P I E J E I A
N S S P B U F Q W A O Y A O T
C U R I O S I T Y S H O P N F
D A V I D J F R I E N D B S Y
```

A Tale Of / Two Cities

Barnaby Rudge

Bleak House

David / Copperfield

Dombey And Son

Great / Expectations

Our Mutual / Friend

Hard Times

Little / Dorrit

Nicholas / Nickleby

Oliver / Twist

The Old / Curiosity Shop

The Pickwick / Papers

ⓘ DID YOU KNOW?

Dickens was working on one final novel, The Mystery of Edwin Drood—about the disappearance of a young man—when he died suddenly in 1870. He left no notes or hints about what he intended the ending to be, so Edwin's mysterious disappearance remains unsolved.

51

Can you fit all 23 of these state capitals into this deconstructed crossword grid, based on nothing more than the number of letters in their name?

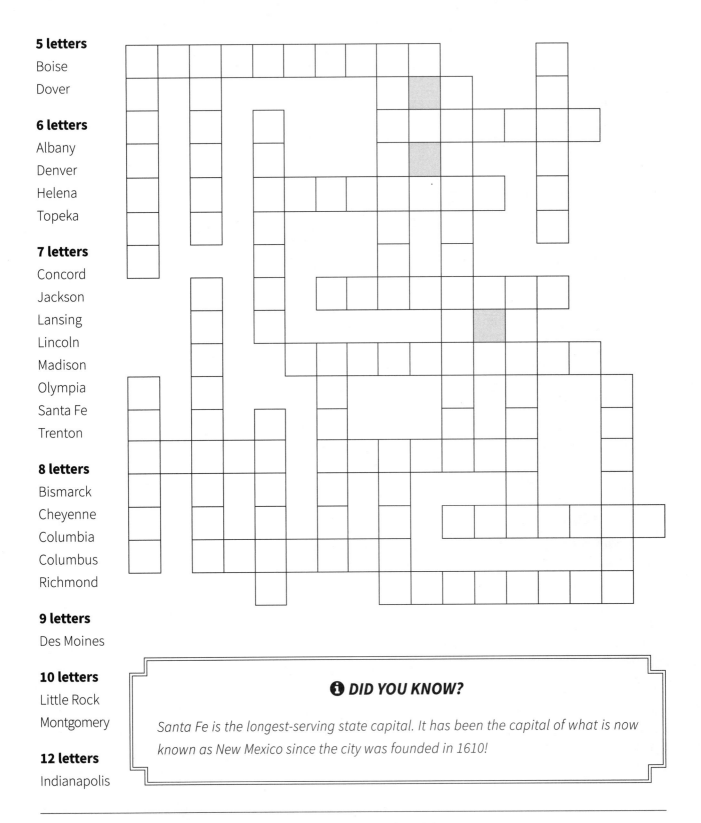

5 letters
Boise
Dover

6 letters
Albany
Denver
Helena
Topeka

7 letters
Concord
Jackson
Lansing
Lincoln
Madison
Olympia
Santa Fe
Trenton

8 letters
Bismarck
Cheyenne
Columbia
Columbus
Richmond

9 letters
Des Moines

10 letters
Little Rock
Montgomery

12 letters
Indianapolis

❶ *DID YOU KNOW?*

Santa Fe is the longest-serving state capital. It has been the capital of what is now known as New Mexico since the city was founded in 1610!

52

1. Well known, like a celebrity
2. Animal that lives in a warren
3. Permits, lets
4. Required
5. Taps on a door
6. France's continent
7. Take a small bite
8. Cold dishes of leafy vegetables
9. Hypothesis
10. Consuming food
11. Spouse's family members
12. Moved the head in agreement
13. Hit, thumped
14. Central
15. Enormous bodies of water
16. Spout
17. Wept
18. Walk softly
19. Breathe out
20. Put back, restore to a former condition

#					
1				U	
2					
3				W	
4					
5					
6					
7		B			
8				D	
9					Y
10					
11			W		
12					
13			U		K
14		D			
15					
16			Z		
17		B			
18		P			
19	X				
20		V			

ⓘ DID YOU KNOW?

The animal in CLUE 2 here is an invasive species in Australia, the threat posed by which became such a problem in the early 1900s that a fence was built across the entire country from north to south. When completed in 1950, the 1,139-mile fence became the longest unbroken manmade barrier in the world.

53

17	7	11	19	12	20	14	23	19	6	4	■	26	4	7
7	■	2	■	23	■	2	■	18	■	26	■	4	■	20
4	18	7	6	17	■	12	7	18	19	12	14	7	12	4
11	■	10	■	7	■	7	■	19	■	12	■	9	■	23
12	20	23	8	12	19	20	17	4	■	7	21	26	20	8
23	■	4	■	■	■	17	■	7	■	6	■	8	■	24
3	7	14	12	20	24	4	■	17	20	17	4	■	■	■
7	■	4	■	18	■	■	■	■	■	7	■	10	■	10
■	■	■	13	19	12	1	■	4	26	12	9	20	11	7
25	■	4	■	8	■	7	■	8	■	■	■	16 (J)	■	20
12	20	14	23	19	■	14	7	7	6	20	25	7 (E)	12	4
20	■	20	■	25	■	11	■	6	■	3	■	4 (S)	■	26
18	26	3	8	23	4	2	7	17	■	19	26	14	7	12
2	■	8	■	22	■	26	■	7	■	15	■	23	■	7
4	7	7	■	7	5	18	7	12	23	7	6	11	7	17

A B C D E F G H I J K L M N O P Q R S T U V W X Y Z

1	2	3	4	5	6	7	8	9	10	11	12	13
14	15	16	17	18	19	20	21	22	23	24	25	26

54

Across

1. Theatrical work (5)

4. Rigid (5)

5. A wizard's incantation (5)

Down

1. School tables (5)

2. Similar (5)

3. Horrible (5)

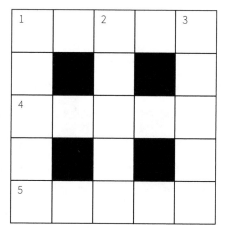

55

1. French number one (2)

2. Almond or pecan, for example (3)

3. Up to the point of (archaic) (4)

4. List numbers in order (5)

5. Tropical bird with a long bill and black and white feathers (6)

6. Sale that goes to the highest bidder (7)

7. Warns, recommends against (8)

8. Dogged, fiercely determined (9)

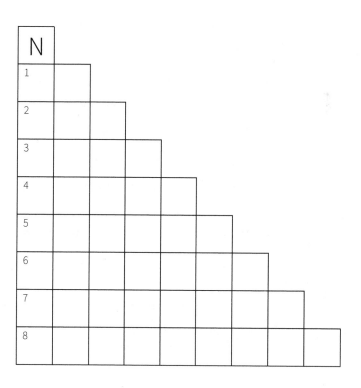

56

All the answers to these questions end in the same two letters. Can you work out what they are?

1. What is struck in a game of badminton?

2. At what landmark did the Pilgrims supposedly disembark from the Mayflower?

3. Who is the patron saint of Ireland?

4. What name is given to a large male adult gorilla?

5. By what name is Australia's Uluru also known?

6. Who played Atticus Finch in the 1962 adaptation of *To Kill A Mockingbird*?

7. What item of sporting equipment is a maximum of 41.3 inches long when played on a field, and 63 inches long when played on ice?

8. What classic Disney character has the middle name Fauntleroy?

9. Who won the Best Actress Oscar for her role in *The Blind Side*?

10. Which Nobel Prize winner wrote the novels *Tortilla Flat* and *Cannery Row*?

11. What is the common name for the golden Islamic shrine found on the Temple Mount in the Old City of Jerusalem?

12. What is the only province of Canada that has both French and English as its official languages?

13. What major cultural event took place August 15-18, 1969, on a dairy farm in Bethel, New York?

14. What form of poetry shares its name with a port city in southwestern Ireland?

15. What Austrian city hosted the 1964 and 1976 Winter Olympics?

16. After Heathrow, what is London's second major international airport?

17. What 1987 Oscar-winning comedy-drama starred Cher, Nicolas Cage, and Olympia Dukakis?

18. Which bestselling doctor wrote *The Common Sense Book of Baby and Child Care* in 1946?

19. Which American artist was known for his "drip technique"?

20. What part of a horse's mane droops down from the "poll" at the top of the head?

---

❶ DID YOU KNOW?

The artist in QUESTION 19 here is responsible for one of the world's most expensive artworks. His 1948 painting Number 17A was bought by hedge fund manager Kenneth C Griffin in 2015 for $200 million. It is currently on display in the Art Institute of Chicago.

57

Across

8. Not intense; regular, normal (8)

9. Put on a play (6)

10. Brave (6)

11. Shook from the cold (8)

12. Abandoned (8)

13. Reply (6)

14. Precious geometric gem (7)

17. Lowest (7)

19. Jagged line (6)

21. Tied, buckled (8)

24. International border (8)

25. Formed (6)

26. Tags (6)

27. After tenth (8)

Down

1. Find (6)

2. Mails to your door (8)

3. Aim (6)

4. Rented (6)

5. Guess (8)

6. Boiled bread rolls (6)

7. Umpires (8)

15. Train track (8)

16. Most furious (8)

18. Readies (8)

20. Crazier (6)

21. Let slip from the mind (6)

22. Female sibling (6)

23. Occurrences, happenings (6)

58

All 30 of the words and names in this grid contain at least one letter Q.

```
C  O  L  L  O  Q  U  Y  Z  N  S  Q  B  K  B
S  U  Q  C  A  Y  S  X  A  S  Q  U  A  L  L
Q  U  I  L  T  L  Q  U  E  R  Y  R  N  S  H
U  N  L  I  C  T  B  U  M  A  C  A  Q  U  E
A  I  U  Q  O  E  Q  U  I  V  O  Q  U  E  A
R  Q  E  U  N  C  U  U  Q  E  U  A  E  A  D
E  U  E  E  S  H  I  B  E  U  T  T  T  R  Q
B  E  C  Y  E  N  T  E  Q  S  E  A  Q  T  U
E  B  O  B  Q  I  E  Z  U  P  T  R  N  H  A
Q  A  A  O  U  Q  W  I  O  I  C  N  Q  Q  R
U  R  Q  U  E  U  E  Q  T  E  E  G  N  U  T
E  O  U  Q  N  E  H  U  E  E  E  I  T  A  E
A  Q  I  U  T  X  O  E  U  B  E  P  G  K  R
T  U  C  E  M  S  E  Q  U  E  N  C  E  E  S
H  E  K  T  A  R  A  B  E  S  Q  U  E  K  E
```

Albuquerque	Bezique	Earthquake	Qatar	Quick	Sequence
Arabesque	Bouquet	Equity	Queen	Quiet	Squall
Banquet	Clique	Equivoque	Query	Quilt	Square
Baroque	Colloquy	Headquarters	Quest	Quite	Technique
Bequeath	Consequent	Macaque	Queue	Quote	Unique

ⓘ DID YOU KNOW?

Q is the least-used letter of the English alphabet, only slightly behind the likes of J, X, and Z. On average, you'll only come across one Q in every 500 letters of English writing—although on this page, that number is slightly higher!

59

This is an anagram acrostic—reshuffle the clue words and put them into the right places in the grid to spell out a hidden word reading downward in the shaded column.

1. Mailers   **6.** Reflows

2. Engrain   **7.** Defiant

3. Creches   **8.** Lactose

4. Holiest   **9.** Salient

5. Haunter   **10.** Bloused

1					M
2			I		
3	C				
4			I		
5					H
6	O				
7			T		
8	C				
9			I		S
10	U				

60

January
February
March
April
May
June
July
August
September
October
November
December

J	S	E	P	T	E	M	B	E	R
U	A	F	E	B	R	U	A	R	Y
N	U	N	Z	T	N	G	R	F	H
E	G	J	U	L	Y	E	P	C	A
C	U	D	V	A	B	Z	R	I	P
O	S	N	J	O	R	A	Y	U	R
Q	T	C	T	E	M	Y	M	I	I
M	G	C	R	U	A	R	O	A	L
N	O	V	E	M	B	E	R	E	Y
D	E	C	E	M	B	E	R	M	C

61

1. Give up the throne (8)

2. Region of Canada; retriever (8)

3. Of a model or painting: very realistic (8)

4. Someone who deliberately tries to ruin an enterprise (8)

5. Area of forest (8)

6. Taught in school (8)

7. Float, hover (8)

8. First Monday in September (5,3)

9. Sporting breaks or momentary pauses in a game (4-4)

10. Small prickly mammal (8)

11. American gangster, jailed in 1931 (2,6)

12. Winter Olympic sled (8)

13. Totally surround (8)

14. Enumerated, gave values to (8)

15. Problems, tricky choices (8)

16. Conjuror, wizard (8)

17. Correction fluid; blizzarding weather (5-3)

18. Knot together (8)

19. Total lack of energy (8)

20. Started a project (8)

	1	2	3	4	5	6	7	8
1	B							
2		B						
3							K	
4		B					U	
5			D					D
6		U						
7		V						
8		B						
9			E					
10								G
11				P				
12				G				
13		C				C		
14		M						
15						M		
16			C					
17	H							T
18						N		
19								Y
20						H		

ⓘ DID YOU KNOW?

The gangster in CLUE 11 here was jailed for tax evasion—despite his rumored involvement in a lengthy series of murders, including the St Valentine's Day Massacre in 1929. He was sentenced to 11 years in jail, and fined $50,000; at the time, it was the harshest sentence ever handed down for tax fraud in US history.

62

			12 F		15		7		12		6			
	20	10	19 L	5	18	26	10		4	18	5	6	22	
	21		18 A		2		17		21		14		6	
18	22	22	15		1	19	18	7	17	4	10	23	26	22
	6		14		19				14				2	
9	10	23	19	22	6	4	15		11	14	4	10	18	11
			21				11		6		6		4	
12	4	10	17		15	14	10	25	26		2	18	8	6
	6		14		23		4				18			
19	18	15	11	6	22		2	18	3	10	4	21	11	7
	19				22				23		8		18	
2	21	15	15	1	6	19	19	6	22		18	24	19	6
	13		10		26		21		17		9		8	
	6	16	23	18	19		26	6	6	22	19	6	15	
			1		7		8		15		6			

A B C D E F G H I J K L M N O P Q R S T U V W X Y Z

1	2	3	4	5	6	7	8	9	10	11	12	13
14	15	16	17	18	19	20	21	22	23	24	25	26

63

This is a double acrostic puzzle! There are two hidden phrases to solve here, one spelled out by the first letters of the answers, the other by their last letters, reading downward in the shaded columns. Work out each one for a bonus point.

1. Brazil's capital (8)

2. Vegetable known as an aubergine in Europe (8)

3. Popular purple or pink-flowering plant (8)

4. Agrees to, lets pass (8)

5. Puts money back into (8)

6. Paper container for a letter in the mail (8)

7. How the animals entered Noah's Ark (3-2-3)

8. Start to get along (3,2,3)

9. Ability to see, sense of vision (8)

10. Very quickly—like lightning! (2,1,5)

11. Rum and citrus cocktail, named for a Cuban village (8)

12. Political vote (8)

13. Talking (8)

14. Covers, hides from view (8)

15. Predict the weather (8)

16. Malarial fly (8)

17. Sporty (8)

18. 1959 John Wayne western (3,5)

19. Metallic element Cr, used to make stainless steel (8)

20. Good-looking (8)

#								
1						I		
2			G					
3		I				I		
4			P					
5				V				
6								
7			B					
8			T			F		
9		Y						
10			F					
11			Q					
12		L						
13				K				
14		B						
15				C				
16			Q					
17			H					
18			O			V		
19				M				
20					O			

64

All these questions have TWO answers. Score yourself one point if you can name one correct answer—but as a bonus, score yourself three points if you can give BOTH answers.

How many points can you score out of a maximum of 45?

1. A standard dictionary will list two mammals whose names begin AA–. What are they?

2. What are the cheapest and most expensive properties on a standard New York Monopoly board?

3. What were the first two Beatles songs to reach Number 1 on the Billboard charts in February and March 1964, respectively?

4. What long-necked waterbird has varieties called mute and whooper, and what other type of long-necked waterbird has varieties called demoiselle and sandhill?

5. What seas do the east and west coasts of England lie on?

6. Cary Grant starred in four Alfred Hitchcock movies, two in the 40s and two in the 50s. *Suspicion* and *Notorious* were the 1940s movies—what were the other two?

7. In a game of tennis, what is a score of 0 known as, and what is a score of 40-40 known as?

8. In a standard game of chess, two pieces are normally limited to moving only one square at a time during play. Which ones?

9. Two letters of the alphabet are marked with a "tittle" when written in lowercase. What are they?

10. California shares most of its land border with neighboring Nevada. What two other states does it border?

11. What classic 1859 novel opens with the line, "It was the best of times, it was the worst of times"? And what classic 1813 novel opens, "It is a truth universally acknowledged, that a single man in possession of a good fortune, must be in want of a wife"?

12. The first and second US vice presidents to take over following the death of the president did so in 1841 and 1850. Who were they?

13. What are the Roman numerals for 100 and 1,000?

14. What are the two European countries whose names begin with F?

15. Who were the two wives of Henry VIII named Anne?

65

Across

6. Chemical equation (7)

7. Companion (7)

9. Bird of prey (5)

10. Fondness (9)

11. Large city (7)

13. Godly (6)

15. Random (13)

19. Oak seeds (6)

20. Pairings (7)

23. Poignant (9)

24. Music speed (5)

26. Olympian (7)

27. Young of 1 down

Down

1. Adult form of 27 ACROSS (4)

2. Most impolite (6)

3. Lines that never meet (9)

4. Rehearse (8)

5. Lone, sole (10)

6. Violently forceful or dangerous (6)

7. A waft of air or powder (4)

8. Expanses of mountains (6)

12. Science of thinking and thought (10)

14. Work out mathematically (9)

16. Ponder (8)

17. Photo-taking device (6)

18. Home from the sea (6)

21. Messy (6)

22. One time (4)

25. Natural satellite (4)

Can you find all 30 of these classic card games in the grid?

```
O L D M A I D C P I Q U E T O
B R I D G E J I H I O M B R E
R O U G E E T N O I R I Q Z T
N S J M B L A C K J A C K B O
Q B Z Z M O A H X Y F A R O G
S A F P N Y P A T I E N C E L
W C X I O V I N G T E T U N W
I C S M C N E C A R T E X X C
T A H E A R T S L C L O C K A
C R N I E S P O I L F I V E N
H A Y K I N A P O L E O N N F
T T O H O L A C A N A S T A I
X P W E U C H R E P S N A P E
S P I D E R B E Z I Q U E G L
B O S T O N A U O T I O N M D
```

Auction	Canasta	Euchre	Patience	Snap
Baccarat	Canfield	Faro	Piquet	Spider
Bezique	Casino	Hearts	Poker	Spoil Five
Blackjack	Cinch	Napoleon	Pontoon	Switch
Boston	Clock	Old Maid	Rouge-et-noir	Vingt-et-un
Bridge	Écarte	Ombre	Rummy	Whist

ⓘ DID YOU KNOW?

The world's oldest surviving playing cards are kept in the Benaki Museum in Athens. They're thought to be more than 800 years old.

67

20	15	7	5	■	23	9	7	18	18
25	■	10	■	1	■	3	■	2	■
8	2	7	21	4	15	25	2	14	3
2	■	10	■	25	■	3	■	25	■
17	■	21	2	6	3	■	2	15	13
9	3	25	■	3	16	2	12	■	7
■	12 T	■	26	■	2	■	12	■	11
15	2 A	19	1	15	4	21	2	20	25
■	18 F	■	24	■	3	■	10	■	15
1	18	12	25	24	■	12	22	7	3

A B C D E F G H I J K L M N O P Q R S T U V W X Y Z

1	2	3	4	5	6	7	8	9	10	11	12	13
14	15	16	17	18	19	20	21	22	23	24	25	26

68

The names of FIVE different keyboard instruments have been jumbled together below, and their letters arranged in alphabetical order. Unjumble the words and fill the instruments' names into the boxes below.

~~A~~ A A A A ~~C~~ C ~~C~~ D D G ~~H~~ H H I I I I ~~M~~ ~~M~~
N N N O O O O O O O ~~P~~ ~~R~~ R R R R S U

| | R | | | | | | P | | C | H | | | | | A | | |

| | | | M | | | M | | C | C | | | | |

What word is this?

_ E _ _ O _ _ I _ I _ I _ Y

1. Prickly desert plant (6)

2. Arm joints (6)

3. Tidier (6)

4. Spoke (6)

5. Beard trimmers (6)

6. Overseas, not in this country (6)

7. Bigger (6)

8. Tight, not much room (6)

9. Fourscore (6)

10. Turn down (6)

11. Seller (6)

12. *The Iceman Cometh* playwright Eugene (6)

13. Together as one, at the same time (6)

14. Struggle against circumstance; work hard (6)

15. Took small amounts of liquid (6)

16. Gaped the mouth with tiredness (6)

17. Nap, short sleep (6)

18. Random information; general knowledge (6)

19. Paris' famous tower (6)

20. Noon (6)

#					
1		C			
2				W	
3		A			
4			K		
5		Z			
6		O			
7		G			
8					W
9					Y
10			U		
11			D		
12					L
13					N
14			V		
15			P		
16		W			
17			Z		
18			V		
19		F			
20				Y	

71

	6		25		10		7		6		20		24	
1	8	24	21		25	21	8	4	26	13	15	2	12	18
	13		8		24		12		4		2		5	
10	23	8	4	6	18		10	2	25	25	13	6	10	10
	22		23		6			23		23				
10	9	2	24	13	13	6	21		24	12	10	6	20	23
	2		19				24		8				22	
22	8	3	6		22	2	19	8	12		20	22	6	14
	5				15		16				8		6	
13	6	17	15	13	19		10	20	22	15	21	8	13	10
			20		6				15		6		17	
17	15	21	21 (L)	15 (O)	14 (W)	6	18		23	15	12	26	2	6
	14		15		15		6		6		18		21	
6	21	6	20	23	13	24	20	8	21		8	11	21	6
	10		5		5		5		10		13		4	

A B C D E F G H I J K L M N O P Q R S T U V W X Y Z

1	2	3	4	5	6	7	8	9	10	11	12	13
14	15	16	17	18	19	20	21	22	23	24	25	26

72

1. A computer's identifying online address (2)

2. Pastry dish, either sweet or savory (3)

3. Of fruit: ready for eating (4)

4. Shallow glass dish, used in laboratories (5)

5. Swashbuckler, criminal seafarer (6)

6. Trudge, walk wearily over distance (7)

7. One who feeds off another (8)

8. Containing very different parts; contrasting (9)

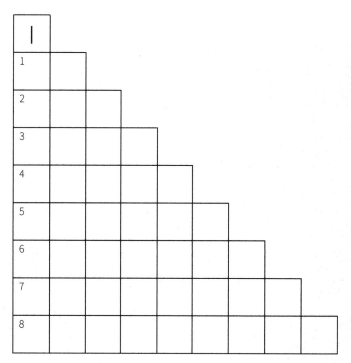

73

This is a mega multijumble! The names of 12 jewels and precious gems have been jumbled up together, and their letters placed in alphabetical order. Can you unjumble them and place the reconstructed names them in the right boxes?

A A A A A A A A A A A B D D D D E̶ E E E E E E G̶ H H
I I I I J̶ J L M M M N N N N O̶ O O O O P̶ P̶ P̶ P̶ P P Q
R R R R R S S S T̶ T T T T U̶ U X Y̶ Y̶ Y̶ Z

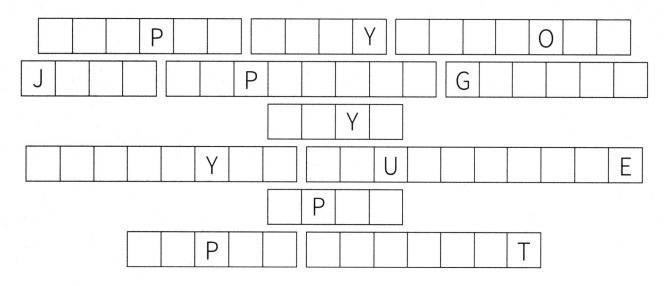

74

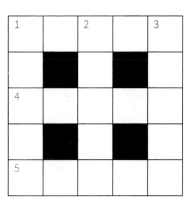

Across

1. Bull (5)

4. Ballots (5)

5. Challenges (5)

Down

1. Rescued (5)

2. Return key (5)

3. Upsurges (5)

75

These questions are tough, but there's a twist—all the answers begin AND end with the letter A. Based on that, see how many of them you can answer correctly…

1. Yerevan is the capital of what former Soviet republic?

2. Which American comic actor—best known for his role in a long-running sitcom—was nominated for an Oscar in 2004 for his role in Martin Scorsese's *The Aviator*?

3. What word for a grand stadium or sports venue derives from the Latin word for sand?

4. The willow ptarmigan is the state bird of where?

5. Who was the Ancient Greek equivalent of the Roman goddess of wisdom, Minerva?

6. In medicine, what is chest pain caused by reduced blood flow to the heart muscles called?

7. What is a fear of spiders known as?

8. Adela Quested is a character in what classic English novel of 1924, which was adapted for cinema by David Lean in 1984?

9. What Caribbean island nation has a sunrise on its flag?

10. The phrase "salad days" comes from a line in what Shakespeare play?

11. What Italian phrase is used to describe singing without a musical accompaniment?

12. What body of what lies between Italy and Croatia?

13. One of the Seven Wonders of the Ancient World, in what Egyptian city was the Pharos built?

14. What South American creature is also known as the water boa?

15. Who won an Oscar for directing *The English Patient*?

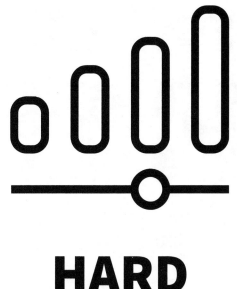

HARD

Let's make things a little trickier!

These puzzles might have some less familiar words,
as well as a few more surprises…

76

Across

1. Financial reports (6)

4. Gains entry (8)

9. Recycles (6)

10. More short-tempered (8)

12. Enormous (4)

13. Instructions (10)

15. Celebrities (12)

18. Likenesses (12)

21. Began (10)

22. The back of the foot (4)

24. Microscopic microorganisms (8)

25. Child, youngster (6)

26. All people (8)

27. Stopped (6)

Down

1. Zeppelins (8)

2. Menial work (8)

3. At that time (4)

5. Reduced to an essence (12)

6. Understanding others' feelings (10)

7. Marine (6)

8. Strain; pressure (6)

11. A state of disrepair (12)

14. Not negatively (10)

16. Mined inorganic substances (8)

17. On your own (8)

19. Two-times (6)

20. Round shape (6)

23. Leg joint (4)

77

```
C I N N A M O N B U T T E R V
C L O V E S D F L O U R I D A
M A C H O C O L A T E R I R N
C O K R N T B S U M E S L I I
R O L E C A N D I E D P E E L
C H L A T I A T C F Y K B D L
M H C O S I A S I R E C A F A
A L E I R S N W N O A I K R E
A R A R L I E Z G S S E I U X
S R C I R U N S E T T R N I T
Y C O O K I N G O I L E G T R
R F S I E V E H U N Q E S S A
U N I F U Q Y S S G C G O U C
P S E L F R A I S I N G D U T
O V E N S H E L F X T S A N K
```

Baking soda	Cloves	Foil	Self-raising
Butter	Coloring	Frosting	Sieve
Cake tin	Cooking oil	Icing	Syrup
Candied peel	Dried fruits	Molasses	Timer
Cherries	Eggs	Oven shelf	Vanilla extract
Chocolate	Flour	Raisins	Yeast
Cinnamon			

ⓘ DID YOU KNOW?

A museum in Vevey in Switzerland houses the world's oldest cake, which was baked for an Ancient Egyptian named Pepionkh, sometime around 2200 BCE!

78

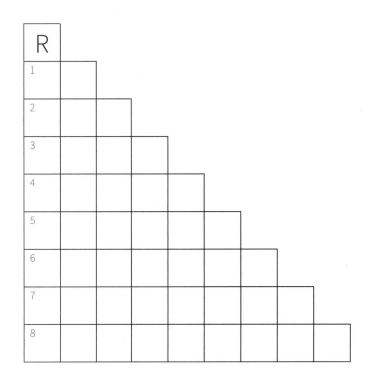

1. Egyptian sun god

2. Auricular organ

3. Shakespearean king

4. Noblemen

5. Signals, warns

6. Deer horns

7. Outdoor toilets

8. Knottiest, most tangled

79

The names of five different types of coffee have been jumbled together here and their letters placed in alphabetical order. Can you unjumble them back into the corresponding boxes below? Some of the letters have been put in the correct places to help…

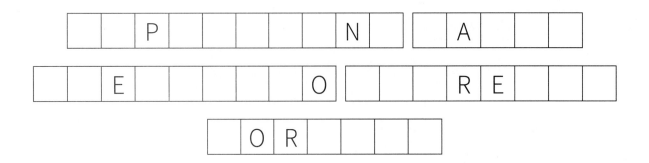

80

1. Cartoon moviemakers

2. Primly, prissily

3. Presaged, foreshadowed

4. Person selected for a role or office

5. Coerce onto a bad course in life (3,6)

6. Later

7. Most ill-humored

8. Domestic; one's own

9. Was bequeathed

10. Uncompromisingly

11. English city on the River Tyne

12. Ruthless

13. Those who eat everything

14. Not cooked enough

15. Dolt, nincompoop

16. Puts up with

17. Jumping out on

18. Insensible

19. Mention directly

20. Undergrowth

#								
1			M					
2		U				H		
3			T					
4				I				
5								Y
6	F							
7			B					
8							W	
9		H						
10			M					
11		W						
12				I				
13	M							
14					D			
15			B		K			
16		L						
17		B						
18		L						
19		M					C	
20				B			R	

❶ DID YOU KNOW?

The city that is the answer to CLUE 11 here is so perfectly positioned on the River Tyne that its 15th century cathedral, St Nicholas' Cathedral, was once used as a lighthouse!

	11	8	19	7	11	11		11	23	13	24	7	26	
	5		5		22		4		14		22		22	
21	13	3	25		2	13	15	13	18	7	2	7	15	8
	2		2		7		24		18		23		1	
11	23	7	7	24	5		22	23	7	19	13	8	7	26
	22				22		2		25		15		25	
5	22	4	11	7	12	14	16	7		3	14	23	11	
			9				22			22				
	24	21	4	7		23	19	7	8	7	15	26	7	26
	22		14		23		8		5				20	
4	2	6	19	7	21	21	13		14	15	17	7	24	8
	23		19		7		6		19		7		4	
10	7	18	7	8	13	6	21	7	11		12	¹⁴I	¹¹S	⁵H
	8		21		11		7		8		7		7	
	7	13	11	14	7	19		24	25	24	21	7	26	

A B C D E F G H I J K L M N O P Q R S T U V W X Y Z

1	2	3	4	5	6	7	8	9	10	11	12	13
14	15	16	17	18	19	20	21	22	23	24	25	26

82

	1		4		21	19	1	14	11
22	25	8	10	7			14		12
	8		6		16	1	13	8	18
18	1	17	10		19		20		9
12		12		2 **J**	12	24	10	1	23
20	8	7	11	1 **A**	9		23		5
1		7		3 **Z**		21	23	8	26
6	1	23	13	3 **Z**		23		14	
4		5			7	1	6	16	15
22	20	19	8	17		17		12	

A	N
B	O
C	P
D	Q
E	R
F	S
G	T
H	U
I	V
J	W
K	X
L	Y
M	Z

1	11	21
2	12	22
3	13	23
4	14	24
5	15	25
6	16	26
7	17	
8	18	
9	19	
10	20	

83

1. Partied

2. Scalier

3. Dyelines

4. Fluents

5. Causers

6. Drayage

7. Emulges

8. Enclave

9. Aitches

10. Alanyls

11. Cilices

12. Algeses

84

Twenty straightforward general knowledge questions to keep you busy!

1. What kind of creature is a swamp moccasin?

2. Who wrote *Murder on the Orient Express*?

3. Also known just as the Antarctic Ocean, what is the name of the ocean that surrounds Antarctica?

4. What is the name of the alphabet used to write the Russian language?

5. Who is the patron saint of lost objects?

6. What traditional Australian song tells the story of "a jolly swagman camped by a billabong"?

7. Which British actor was nominated for an Oscar for his title role in 1963's *Tom Jones*?

8. Xerxes the Great the ruled which ancient nation in the 5th century BCE?

9. What do you do when you "sternutate"?

10. What item of track and field athletic equipment weights 16 lbs for men and 8.8 lbs for women?

11. What is the full name of the dog breed popularly known as a "Westie"?

12. What part of a tree is used to make cork?

13. In what century did Queen Anne reign in England?

14. In what European capital is the Pompidou Centre?

15. What is a muntjac?

16. Where on the body would a fez be worn?

17. What vegetable is also known as a courgette?

18. Who starred opposite Catherine Zeta Jones in 1999's *Entrapment*?

19. What is the belt that ties a kimono called?

20. What part of the body is also known as the oxter or axilla?

---

❶ *DID YOU KNOW?*

The Pompidou Centre is one of Europe's most impressive mixed cultural landmarks, and houses a library of 500,000 books and 50,000 artworks. But its outside appearance is not quite so popular with its locals, and it's often compared to a boilerhouse!

85

Across

1. Otherwise (6)

6. Dispensed liquid (6)

10. Blocks of bread (6)

11. Experiencing solitude (6)

12. Nasty (5)

13. Speediest (7)

15. Communicated with the hands (6)

17. Thought (4)

19. Resounding sound (4)

21. Kayaks (6)

23. Broad smile (4)

24. Put faith in (7)

26. Producer (12)

29. Most used language (7)

32. Container for flowers (4)

33. Glass in the wall of a house (6)

35. Perishes (4)

36. Not this (4)

38. Keyboard instruments (6)

40. Blanketed (7)

41. Group of people (5)

43. Vocal works for the stage (6)

44. Parts of a play (6)

45. Heaps, untidy areas (6)

46. Having unkempt hair (6)

Down

2. Neither (3)

3. Chortling (8)

4. Level; fair (4)

5. Choose (6)

6. Unadorned (5)

7. Undoes a knot (6)

8. Rushes, thick grasses (5)

9. Otherwise (4)

14. Yell (5)

15. Portion of an orange (7)

16. Digital information (4)

18. House details (7)

20. Tall lifting machine on a building lot (5)

22. Honking waterbirds (5)

25. Practicing (8)

27. Thinner, slenderer (5)

28. Cut with a knife or ax (4)

30. Units of liquid volume (6)

31. Swap (6)

33. Undulations of the sea (5)

34. Put on clothes (5)

37. Wish or long for (4)

39. Region (4)

42. Beseech (3)

86

```
A T U G E T C G M O U N T A I N N
D D P O R F A R R E H S A R H T
I E M L O L C O D H N H G R G D
W N E D M I T U W W L B P T D T
I I A F I C U S Y L L H R E G S
S B D I T K S E U U E E F R B D
L O O N L E W G E A M F W O L N
A R W C A R R H S M U A W A J N
N H L H B J E A A R J M I D L L
D E A D U N N H F I Y E L R N A
R L R G G T W K U O E R L U D N
E O K B R O W N Y L B I O N E I
D I K J L E I I O T I C W N D D
J R D L P E L I C A N A E E O R
E O E P T A R M I G A N U R H A
L Y F L Y C A T C H E R U Q R C
```

American / Robin

Baltimore / Oriole

Blue hen

Brown / Thrasher

Cactus wren

Cardinal

Flicker

Flycatcher

Goldfinch

Gull

Loon

Meadowlark

Nene

Pelican

Pheasant

Quail

Rhode / Island Red

Roadrunner

Ruffed / Grouse

Willow / Ptarmigan

Yellowhammer

ⓘ *DID YOU KNOW?*

The first state birds were selected in 1927. The last state to choose its official state bird was Arizona, which selected the cactus wren in 1973. The northern cardinal is the state bird of seven states.

87

Can you work out where all the numbers from one to twenty sit in this grid?

3 letters
One
Six
Ten
Two

4 letters
Five
Four
Nine

5 letters
Eight
Seven
Three

6 letters
Eleven
Twelve
Twenty

7 letters
Fifteen
Sixteen

8 letters
Eighteen
Fourteen
Nineteen
Thirteen

9 letters
Seventeen

88

1. Smallest state
2. Anger
3. Ceremony, ritual
4. Attempter
5. Cease working
6. Redraft
7. More diluted
8. Potent liquor

89

1. Breathe noisily

2. Cure-all; magical potion

3. Fluid

4. Pianist composer of the "Raindrop Prelude"

5. Foreseer

6. Emblem

7. White fur of a stoat

8. Draw unthinkingly

9. Author

10. Damage, harm

11. Most well behaved; mildest

12. Truthful

13. Beginning

14. Miners

15. One or the other

16. Pleasantest

17. Reply

18. Turn against; uprise

19. Desert hallucination

20. Detective

ⓘ DID YOU KNOW?

Despite being one of the most popular and celebrated composers in the world, the answer to CLUE 4, was painfully shy and only gave around 30 performances in his lifetime—and every time, he would request all light be extinguished in the room so he could play unseen in the dark!

#					
1				Z	
2			X		
3		Q			
4			P		
5			C		
6			C		
7		M			
8					E
9			T		
10		P			
11		M			
12					T
13		T			T
14		T			N
15			H		
16		C			
17			W		
18		V			
19				G	
20			U		

A B C D E F G H I J K L M N O P Q R S T U V W X Y Z

1	2	3	4	5	6	7	8	9	10	11	12	13
14	15	16	17	18	19	20	21	22	23	24	25	26

91

What word is this?

TH _ U _ _ _ _ TH

92

Across

1. Saintly biography (11)

7. Fail to interpret correctly (11)

8. Distends, balloons (6)

9. Surrounded by (4)

11. Toothed item for untangling hair (4)

12. Spikes, tines (6)

15. Glorious (11)

16. Doubt, reservation (11)

Down

1. Finds a dwelling for (5)

2. Devout songs (6,5)

3. *Lawrence of Arabic* star Peter (6)

4. Unthinkingly quick to act (4)

5. A blended word (11)

6. Surrender (5)

10. Tiny Bornean sultanate (6)

11. Short-legged Welsh dog breed (5)

13. Erik, French composer of the famous Gnossiennes for piano (5)

14. Smudge, fade together (4)

93

The names of five cold weather events have been jumbled together here. Can you unjumble them into the correct boxes below?

A̶ A A A B C D D E̶ E E F H H H̶ I I I L̶
N̶ N O O R R S T T T U̶ V W W Z Z

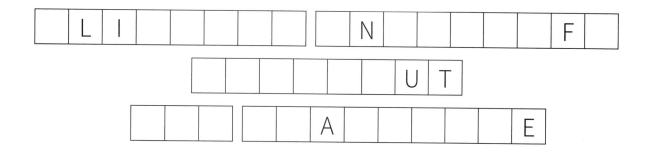

| | L | I | | | | | | | N | | | | F | |

| | | | | | U | T |

| | | | | A | | | | | E | |

94

The answers to these seven questions all have something in common—work out what that is for a bonus eighth point!

1. What word for a monumental tomb derives from the name of an ancient king?

2. What New York venue is known by the initial MSG?

3. Who was the Greek goddess of the hunt?

4. 1/3 × base area × height is the formula for finding the volume of what solid shape?

5. What is the state capital of Washington?

6. What was the title of the only collection of poetry Sylvia Plath published in her lifetime?

7. What kind of building might have a lantern room?

8. What connects all seven of these answers?

95

This is a dominoes game! The 10 six-letter tiles below can be placed into the grid on the left, so that the names of 10 six-letter colors can be read across the rows. One of the letters has been put in place to get you started. Can you complete the grid?

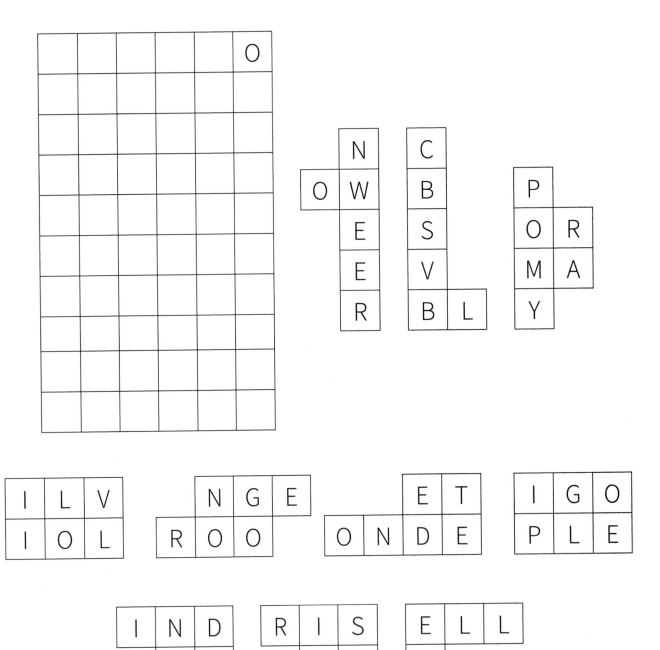

96

Across

6. Alternative, different (5)

7. Not skilled (8)

10. Waiting, still to be dealt with (7)

11. Worker's protective headgear (4,3)

12. Haul, carry with great effort (7)

13. Booty, stolen treasure (7)

14. Unassailable, impossible to defeat (11)

19. Unwieldy (7)

21. Raised a glass (7)

23. Erased (7)

25. Try (7)

26. Instinctual; deep-seated in the body (8)

27. Serve food for (5)

Down

1. Force onto a ship's crew (8)

2. Extol (6)

3. Horizontal span of an aircraft from tip to tip (10)

4. Netting (4)

5. Curved (6)

6. Be against (6)

8. Upset (7)

9. Tempest (5)

13. Done on time (10)

15. Problematic manmade substance (7)

16. Guess (8)

17. Resilient (5)

18. Newspaper boss (6)

20. Temperature scale (6)

22. Escapades (6)

24. Dweeb (4)

97

Some of the world's airports are listed in the grid. Can you find them all?

```
G  Y  D  E  N  N  E  K  S  P  E  K  E  K  G
Y  R  M  I  R  A  B  E  L  S  L  U  U  F  A
G  E  U  B  A  A  M  O  C  A  T  W  Y  J  T
A  A  A  B  N  D  H  A  R  Y  K  R  E  K  I
T  D  T  D  M  T  N  O  M  U  D  S  D  T  R
W  N  E  E  O  A  J  N  D  B  H  L  N  O  A
I  A  G  L  R  N  H  O  R  A  I  R  I  V  N
C  L  E  M  B  R  L  O  N  W  U  S  E  A  Y
K  R  L  D  H  I  M  N  E  H  S  S  Z  L  L
N  A  G  O  L  M  O  L  M  Y  V  C  E  E  U
L  G  O  N  A  N  D  B  A  L  E  H  I  T  A
S  S  S  L  S  I  D  L  P  R  N  I  Z  T  P
E  L  M  D  S  W  D  O  L  O  I  P  A  A  T
B  Y  K  O  V  O  L  A  I  D  C  O  I  U  S
I  U  B  E  N  R  O  F  N  S  E  L  L  U  D
```

Arlanda	Ezeiza	Kerkyra	Orly	St Paul
Bromma	Fornebu	Logan	Oslo	Tacoma
Bromna	Gatwick	Maplin	Rhoose	Tegel
Bykovo	Hamburg	Mirabel	Roissy	
Dulles	Hurn	Nadi	Schipol	Valetta
Dumont	Idlewild	Narita	Shannon	Venice
Dyce	JFK	O'Hare	Speke	Yeadon
Elmdon	Kennedy			

98

Can you find the correct home in the grid for all these terms from language, literature, and linguistics?

3 letter words
Ode
Pun

4 letter words
Case
Coda
Foot
Iamb

Myth
Past
Plot
Poem
Tone

5 letter words
Comma
Essay

Index
Maxim
Novel
Prose
Tense

6 letter words
Dative
Monody

Neuter
Period
Phrase
Pidgin
Stress
Suffix

7 letter words
Digraph

Polemic
Present
Refrain

8 letter words
Anaphora
Epigraph
Rhetoric
Threnody

9 letter word
Adjective

10 letter words
Definition
Petrarchan

13 letter word
Interrogative

99

1. Spicy Mexican sauce

2. Hefty, sizeable

3. Giving one's opinion, suggesting

4. Bewitch, entrance

5. Encroach

6. Blocks out from a text

7. Touching with an absorbent cloth

8. Tested, tried out

9. Decoratively shave or carve wood

10. Not permissible

11. Make less loose

12. Relating to the liver

13. In front of a theatrical audience (2, 5)

14. Stinging plants

15. Those who shorten and proof texts

16. Irons, flattens

17. Small glasses of liquor

18. Seahawks

19. Critique fussily

20. River mouth

#						
1						O
2				H		
3	P					
4			U			
5		P				
6				C		
7			B			
8		M				
9				T		
10		V				
11			H			
12		P				
13	N				G	
14				L		
15					R	
16					H	
17			P			
18	S					
19						K
20			U			

ⓘ DID YOU KNOW?

The bird that is the answer to CLUE 18 here is one of the few migratory birds of prey. In its lifetime, a single bird can fly more than 160,000 miles!

100

■	2	13	2	8	21	10	■	26	2	19	19	25	13	■
25	■	9	■	14	■	2	■	25	■	10	■	20	■	19
9	25	21	8	5	■	4	10	6	25	18	5	21	19	25
10	■	3	■	23	■	21	■	6	■	3	■	6	■	2
13	14	3	21	10	14	4	6	15	■	21	13	25	2	6
25	■	6	■	12	■	■	■	9	■	■	■	15	■	10
4	7	25	25	12	21	25	■	10	20	25	9	25	2	12
■	2	■	10	■	15	■	■	6	■	24	■	■	16	■
25	24	1 P	5 U	14 N	8	25	■	6	2	23	14	5	2	4
5	■	10	■	■	■	4	■	■	■	22	■	10	■	25
13	25	18	10	3	■	22	10	12	22	25	2	13	25	13
25	■	1	■	2	■	2	■	2	■	11	■	4	■	2
2	9	25	2	23	10	13	25	4	■	14	3	10	2	12
9	■	21	■	10	■	10	■	25	■	25	■	17	■	25
■	18	21	5	5	10	7	■	9	2	9	25	17	15	■

A B C D E F G H I J K L M N O P Q R S T U V W X Y Z

1	2	3	4	5	6	7	8	9	10	11	12	13

14	15	16	17	18	19	20	21	22	23	24	25	26

101

Across

1. Where unopened mail goes (5)

4. Cults, tight-knit communities (5)

7. A lowing of a cow (3)

8. Stretchy fabric (5)

9. Group of eight musicians (5)

10. Stank (6)

11. Make a picture smaller (4)

13. Disgust with excessive sweetness (4)

14. One who disbelieves (6)

17. Greek letter (5)

18. Egg-shaped (5)

19. Metal mixed with copper to make bronze (3)

20. Long, narrow mountaintop or crest (5)

21. Windy (5)

Down

1. Layabout (5)

2. Single's gentleman's pied-à-terre (8,3)

3. Festive seasons (abbrev.) (6)

4. Imminently (4)

5. Sharing the same boundary (11)

6. Arrange; format, configuration (5)

12. Be the property of (6)

13. Seat (5)

15. Red-complexioned (5)

16. Despise (4)

102

What word is this?

_ O _ J U _ _ _ E

103

Another set of 26 questions, one for every letter of the alphabet.

A B C D E F G H I J K L M N O P Q R S T U V W X Y Z

1. What nationality is tennis star Rafael Nadal?

2. Cinnabar is a shade of what color?

3. What kind of animal has species called sloth, Kodiak, and spectacled?

4. What is a curving, sinuous river course known as?

5. What are lady's slipper, nun's hood, and dancing-lady?

6. What is the medical name for the thighbone?

7. What Louisianan city is known as "The Heart of Cajun Country"?

8. Who is the eldest child of Queen Elizabeth II?

9. By what name was the Democratic Republic of the Congo known until 1997?

10. What famous scientist was born in the German city of Ulm in 1879?

11. What is a cat-o'-nine-tails?

12. What is the second-largest country in South America?

13. What name is shared by the playwright Pinter and British prime minister McMillan?

14. Who is the mother of four children named North, Saint, Chicago, and Psalm?

15. What is pain isolated to a single nerve known as?

16. Croatia broke away from what former "Eastern Bloc" republic in the 1990s?

17. Whose hit singles include "Private Dancer" and "The Best"?

18. What children's fictional character hails from "Darkest Peru"?

19. Goa is a major port city in what country?

20. What company developed the first plain paper photocopier in 1969?

21. Who is the father of Absalom in the Bible?

22. What is the second-least-populated US state, after Wyoming?

23. In what month is Twelfth Night celebrated?

24. In what South American nation did the world's first FIFA World Cup take place?

25. What 1990s science-fiction series starred Scott Bakula as Dr. Sam Beckett?

26. Whose law states that "bad money drives out good"?

ⓘ DID YOU KNOW?

As popular as the World Cup is today—with dozens of teams taking part from all across the globe—when the first FIFA competition was held in July 1930, only 13 countries took part!

104

Across

1. They're used on envelopes (7,6)

10. Icehouse (5)

11. Hot-water clothes press (5,4)

12. Comical neologism (5,4)

13. Performing, carrying out (5)

14. Italian rice dish (7)

16. A temporary shelter or fortification (7)

18. Extract (7)

20. Retain for use in the future (7)

22. Infective agent (5)

24. Standard TV broadcast (4-2-3)

26. Momentary pause in hostilities (5-4)

27. Female (5)

28. A worsening course of action (8,5)

Down

2. Rectangles (7)

3. Driver-and-passenger vehicle (3-6)

4. Energy, vigor (5)

5. Narrower, thinner (9)

6. Targeted (5)

7. The surrounding area (7)

8. Crockery (6,7)

9. Medieval chivalrous wanderers (7-6)

15. Inappropriate, not following the rules (3,2,4)

17. Kitchen cloth (4,5)

19. Panacea (4-3)

21. Driver's guide (4,3)

23. Use a broom (5)

25. Each (5)

105

This wordsearch of poets contains a hidden phrase. Once all the words are found, read all the unused letters in order—left to right, top to bottom—to spell out a famous line of poetry written by one of the names on this list. Name that poet for a bonus point!

```
T  N  O  S  N  I  K  C  I  D  E  C  W  R  N
O  A  S  T  A  E  Y  R  O  L  U  A  O  D  I
S  M  E  E  N  O  T  L  I  M  O  S  D  B  K
N  T  H  T  I  P  V  O  M  W  S  E  R  L  R
A  I  G  N  G  N  T  I  E  E  E  T  D  A  A
L  H  U  O  O  I  N  N  T  A  D  N  A  K  L
L  W  H  R  A  G  W  T  N  O  O  L  D  E  A
I  N  Y  B  S  D  I  G  I  I  T  O  I  T  K
M  B  S  H  A  K  E  S  P  E  A  R  E  W  L
C  O  K  I  P  L  I  N  G  K  T  N  H  T  L
M  E  N  O  O  S  S  A  S  O  N  N  S  H  O
E  L  E  U  D  N  U  O  P  Y  S  O  S  O  R
T  R  A  H  T  R  O  W  S  D  R  O  W  M  R
V  E  D  O  N  N  E  O  L  F  E  D  B  A  A
H  T  A  L  P  Y  N  Y  E  L  L  E  H  S  C
```

Angelou	Dickinson	Kipling	Poe	Tennyson
Blake	Donne	Larkin	Pound	Thomas
Bronte	Eliot	McMillan	Rossetti	Whitman
Byron	Frost	Milton	Sassoon	Wilde
Carroll	Hughes	Owen	Shakespeare	Wordsworth
Cummings	Keats	Plath	Shelley	Yeats

	14		10		7	18	2	13	4
19	20	7	18	2			19		2
	13		1		5	8	20	2	8
3	13	25	16		2		4		17
5		20		13	3	1 (L)	3 (A)	24 (M)	20
2	12	22	18	1	21		19		18
12		25		6		11	25	18	24
6	23	17	6	26		25		13	
20		6			21	2	9	2	8
5	8	16	1	16		15		5	

A B C D E F G H I J K L M N O P Q R S T U V W X Y Z

1	2	3	4	5	6	7	8	9	10	11	12	13
14	15	16	17	18	19	20	21	22	23	24	25	26

107

The names of SIX marsupials have been jumbled together below, and their letters arranged in alphabetical order. Unjumble the words and fill the animals names into the boxes below.

A̶A̶ A A A A A A A A B B D E G H̶ I K K L̶ L L L
M̶M̶ M N̶ N N O̶ O O O O P R S S S T T U̶ V W W Y

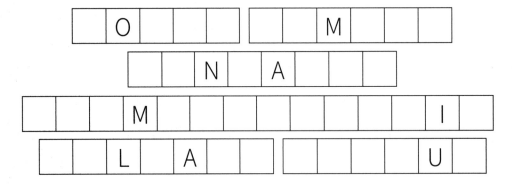

1. Routinely, usually

2. Existing everywhere

3. These Boys had a 90s hit with "Everybody"

4. Shamelessness, boldness

5. Mazes

6. Enfranchising, emboldening

7. Make a room impermeable to noise

8. Bewilderment, confusion

9. Leaving, jettisoning

10. Revealing a shameful truth

11. Prevaricate, speak vaguely or noncommittally

12. Upside down, random (5-5)

13. Zeal

14. Solitude

15. Houdini's field of magic

16. Having a muted, pleasant voice (4-6)

17. Held a party for

18. Bizarre, extraordinary

19. Especially brilliant, remarkable

20. Stretchiness

#									
1		B							Y
2			Q						
3			K				E		
4			Z						
5			Y						
6	M				E				
7								O	F
8			P			X			
9	B								
10			F						
11	Q			V					
12				Y					Y
13				U					M
14		N						S	
15		C							Y
16		F					K		
17				B					
18	U								H
19	H				M				
20			S			C			

	3		5		18		17		22		25		24	
23	18	1	10		8	7	24	3	24	16	10	8	5	24
	25		6		3		8		24		8		10	
8	10	26	1	9	5		23	1	5	24	19	12	21	5
	5		26		24					24				
14	8	20	24		10	3	8	7	1	14	24	11	9	24
	14		11		8		16		11				8	
10	1	24	14		23	18	1	22	22		15	1	11	16
	20				24		14		6		12		5	
14	24	24	10	22	3	24	24	20	24		11	24	24	14
			6						16		4		2	
9 C	25 A	26 T	25	9	8	17	13		1	11	22	6	12	16
	6		9		25		12		13		8		24	
24	19	8	1	5	26	1	9	25	6		8	1	11	4
	25		14		18		4		24		14		26	

A B C D E F G H I J K L M N O P Q R S T U V W X Y Z

1	2	3	4	5	6	7	8	9	10	11	12	13

14	15	16	17	18	19	20	21	22	23	24	25	26

110

In this tricky game, you're given a clue word on the left, and a numbered clue on the right.

The answer to the clue on the right will contain all the letters of the word on the left EITHER plus OR minus one more. Put this extra letter into the numbered box provided.

So the answer to clue one is PRISTINE—which contains all the letters of TIPSIER, plus an extra N, which has been entered into the grid. Can you solve all the clues and the anagrams, so that a 15-letter word reads down the boxes?

#	Clue word	Box	Clue
1.	Tipsier	¹N	Extremely clean _____
2.	Cranium	2	Cosmetic procedure for the hands _____
3.	Printer	3	Shelled water-dwelling reptile _____
4.	Bundle	4	An embarrassing mistake _____
5.	Wasps	5	Dogs' feet _____
6.	Parcel	6	An exact copy _____
7.	Thinly	7	Occurring every evening _____
8.	Writhes	8	Puts pen to paper _____
9.	Pausal	9	Kitchen utensil _____
10.	Elven	10	Number on a soccer team _____
11.	Boomer	11	Tediousness _____
12.	Cadre	12	Ballerina _____
13.	Science	13	Picturesque _____
14.	Kissing	14	Downhill winter sport _____
15.	Strapline	15	Airplane with three sets of wings _____

111

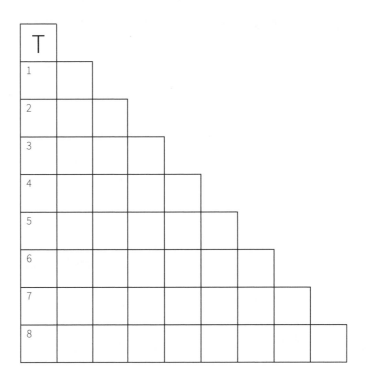

1. Latin "and"

2. Tolkien's talking tree

3. Adolescent

4. Feasted

5. Cancel out

6. Poised, graceful

7. Knot together

8. Sophisticated male

112

Something connects the answers to these 10 questions. What is it? Work it out for a bonus point!

1. What tool can be claw, reflex, ball pein, and sledge?

2. What is the outer color of an archery target?

3. Who directed Boris Karloff in the 1930s movies *Frankenstein* and *The Bride of Frankenstein*?

4. What kind of creature is Shere Khan in *The Jungle Book*?

5. How is Tȟatȟáŋka Íyotake better known?

6. What creatures run Gringotts Wizarding Bank in the *Harry Potter* stories?

7. What comedy drama series starred Edie Falco as an emergency medic?

8. What fruit is baked in the center of a traditional Sussex pond pudding?

9. What stretches for 1,400 miles in the Coral Sea?

10. What vast Arctic island is an autonomous self-governing territory of the kingdom of Denmark?

11. What type of fish goes through lifecycle stages called alevin, fry, parr, and smolt?

12. What connects all 11 of these answers?

113

Unjumble the words on below and place them in the corresponding rows in the grid on the left to spell out a hidden phrase reading down.

1. Redtails

2. Manliest

3. Idolater

4. Dilatory

5. Antinome

6. Antiquer

7. Tempuras

8. Rybaulds

9. Articles

10. Bleating

11. Dateline

12. Dishware

114

What word is this?

__ __ W __ M __ W __ __

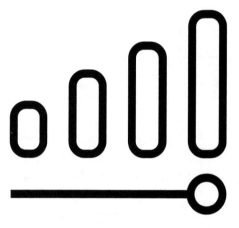

EXPERT

Let's up the ante a little for this last set of games and puzzles!

115

Across

7. Population surveys (8)

9. Slow musical movement (6)

10. Enclosure (4)

11. Stubborn, obstinate (10)

12. Infectious fever (6)

14. Casino wheel (8)

15. Fast-growing woody grass (6)

16. Giant Arctic mammal (6)

19. Redacted, cut (8)

21. Gradually weakened, leeched strength from (6)

23. Musical quaver (6,4)

24. Unclothed (4)

25. Closer (6)

26. Giving in (8)

Down

1. What is left behind (6)

2. Land surrounded by water (4)

3. Strong coffee shot (8)

4. Ideal, idyllic place (6)

5. Rickety old vehicle (10)

6. Moves around the world (8)

8. Trek (6)

13. Half of the globe (10)

15. Direct routes (8)

17. Replied (8)

18. Stupidity (6)

20. Take on again (6)

22. Wrong; culpable (6)

24. Attempts to buy at auction (4)

116

N-y questions? All the words in this grid begin and end with the letter N.

```
N O I T A C I F I T O N U F N
N F B N A H T A N R U O H L U
A O N I G E R I A N R N K O O
M N O I T A Z I L A R U T A N
E I I Y B L N A P O L E O N N
L K H T I N I E N N D C E U N
B P N O R U E N O N U W B O A
O A M E N A S I O N T I E N M
N N E G O R T I N O A N G O R
N I X O N A T I N N Y S T G O
O N O I T A I T O G E N S G N
O Y J C N E L S O N W W T I U
N G I N O V A T I O N P M N N
M N Y L O N P N O T I O N A E
N O T A T I O N N E U T R O N
```

Nan	Negotiation	Newton	Nobleman	Notion
Napkin	Nein	Nictation	Noggin	Noun
Napoleon	Nelson	Nigerian	Non	Novation
Nasion	Neon	Nissan	Noon	Nubian
Nathan	Neuron	Nitration	Norman	Nun
Nation	Neutron	Nitrogen	Notation	Nylon
Naturalization	Newman	Nixon	Notification	

ⓘ DID YOU KNOW?

The letter N gets its familiar up-and-down shape because it derives historically from an Egyptian hieroglyph represented by a snake!

117

Here's a tricky game with lots of potential confusables! All the words that need to be placed back into this grid have six letters, and all of them contain the letters E, F, and G… Good luck!

Beflag	Effigy	Fangle	Finger	Fogger	Gaffer	Griffe
Befogs	Engulf	Feague	Fledge	Forage	Ganefs	Guffie
Begift	Fadged	Feeing	Fledgy	Forego	Goffer	Reflag
Begulf	Fadges	Feigns	Flugel	Fumage	Gonefs	Refuge
Defang	Fanega	Fidged	Fodgel	Gaffed	Griefs	Regift
Defogs	Fanged	Fidget				

118

1. Lottery prizes

2. Unusual, out of the ordinary

3. Imitate, replicate

4. Tenant

5. Unsubtly mention people

6. Took ownership of; gained

7. One who lives next door

8. Piously, showing deep religious dedication

9. Long, slender laboratory glass (4,4)

10. Main text of a front page

11. Forever

12. Come or put together

13. Written proofs of sale

14. Explanatory guide to the words in a book

15. Things that happen as a result of something else

16. Chief gas of air

17. Vexing

18. Messily

19. Actor

20. Most inclined

#							
1				P			
2	B						
3		M	U				
4				P			T
5							P
6		Q					
7				B			
8		V					
9						B	
10				L			
11							Y
12	S						
13		C		P			
14		L					Y
15	U						
16				O			
17				Y			
18		T					
19				P			
20		E			E		

119

17	23	25 A	2 R	22 B	6	■	16	3	1	22	20	23	1	26
3	■	20	■	1	■	■	■	2	■	20	■	24	■	2
19	2	23	23	11	23	■	22	25	22	1	4	8	13	25
2	■	8	■	11	■	4	■	21	■	23	■	1	■	5
5	9	3	17	■	14	25	21	23	2	18	1	10	26	4
20	■	1	■	16	■	19	■	■	■	25	■	23	■	23
20	1	4	21	6	■	25	12	23	17	9	6	■	■	■
4	■	23	■	4	■	2	■	9	■	13	■	8	■	4
■	■	4	26	2	5	21	11	■	23	24	5	4	21	
3	■	12	■	2	■	■	■	23	■	21	■	12	■	3
26	25	2	20	3	2	12	25	10	23	■	9	8	5	9
25	■	3	■	4	■	3	■	25	■	18	■	18	■	13
7	1	3	21	5	23	17	21	■	15	5	9	1	17	25
1	■	15	■	1	■	23	■	■	■	15	■	10	■	16
23	15	23	2	10	3	2	23	■	14	23	23	26	5	23

A B C D E F G H I J K L M N O P Q R S T U V W X Y Z

1	2	3	4	5	6	7	8	9	10	11	12	13
14	15	16	17	18	19	20	21	22	23	24	25	26

120

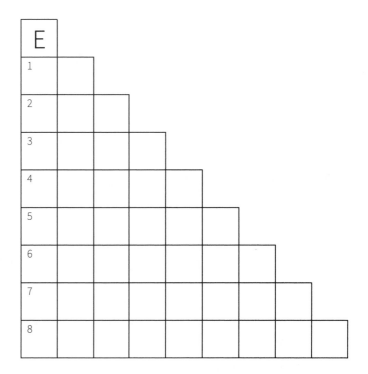

1. Direct opposite of SW

2. 1/100th of a Japanese yen

3. Headland

4. Feel, experience

5. Reduce

6. Eternal

7. Laziness

8. Pushes away; the edges of a football pitch

121

11498	54370
19863	55621
22368	63587
30214	69841
32065	76502
32687	77650
34580	86104
36840	86504
36985	86790
37901	90375
40258	93457
41205	00205
53938	

4	3	6	8	4	0	1	6	8	2
0	1	1	7	8	5	3	6	0	2
0	0	2	0	5	6	6	5	6	3
9	4	4	0	9	7	6	0	7	6
7	1	0	1	3	7	0	9	2	8
6	2	5	2	1	8	3	3	9	3
8	0	6	9	5	4	3	7	0	9
3	5	8	4	5	8	9	6	3	3
2	6	3	7	3	2	6	8	7	5
3	6	9	8	4	1	2	6	5	5

122

All the answers to these questions begin with the same letter…

1. In what 1949 comedy movie did Alex Guinness play nine members of the same family?

2. What children's toy has a name that literally means "viewer of beautiful things"?

3. What state split from Virginia to become the 15th state of the Union in 1792?

4. The male of what mammal is nicknamed a boomer, and the female a flyer?

5. Afognak is the second-largest island in what Alaskan archipelago?

6. What classic television and movie character has a nephew called Robin?

7. What major sporting event was first held on May 17, 1875?

8. What musical instruments are also known as timpani?

9. What is the world's largest lizard?

10. Who won an Oscar for his performance in A Fish Called Wanda?

…and all these answers end in that letter!

11. Which famous explorer was killed in Hawaii in 1779?

12. What classic 1938 Graham Greene novel features the character Pinkie Brown?

13. What was the highest-grossing movie of 1993?

14. "You should've heard them knocked out jailbirds sing" is a line from what song?

15. What poem by Alexander Pope begins "What dire offence from am'rous causes springs"?

16. Who composed a famous suite of Music for Strings, Percussion and Celesta in 1936?

17. Who directed *Dial M for Murder*?

18. Who is the second of the New Testament evangelists?

19. What is the largest city in New Jersey?

20. What Soviet human spaceflight project ran from 1961-63?

ℹ️ DID YOU KNOW?

The director in 17 question wanted an extreme closeup of a finger dialing M on a rotary telephone to open his film, but the 3D cameras in use at the time wouldn't focus on the image correctly. So, to get around it, he had a gigantic wooden finger and proper telephone made!

123

Across

1. Previously said (14)

10. Jewel headband (5)

11. Fortunes, fates (9)

12. Financial investigator (7)

13. Creep like a snake (7)

14. Abdominal crunch (3,2)

16. Suitable or popular enough for public office (9)

19. Gymnastic (9)

20. Dig deep into (5)

22. Salty tinned fish (7)

25. Most proximate (7)

27. Fetcher (9)

28. Gold bar (5)

29. Of an electric device: blew, stopped working (5-9)

Down

2. Trickster, deceiver (9)

3. Poke fun at (5)

4. Most recent or up to date (9)

5. Birds' homes (5)

6. Instigated (9)

7. Whinny (5)

8. Warrant (7)

9. Drinking tubes (6)

15. Promoter (9)

17. Unusual, unlike others (9)

18. Large white-headed bird of prey (4,5)

19. Soaks up (7)

21. Being (6)

23. Fashionably old-fashioned (5)

24. A short concluding stanza or verse (5)

26. Proof that you were elsewhere at the time of a crime (5)

124

The names of 28 characters and creatures from Tolkien's *Lord of the Rings* stories are hidden in this grid.

```
R T A M A E B K C I U Q W N L
R E W M S H A D O W F A X R U
N O M W I A L E G O L A S O G
J F H O R S O F L I M G G Z
I U G T E W G A A S D E O A A
D U W A E E A L R A A R L R N
R B E O N S C A U B R L A G
A J O I R D E H M R M Y U A A
E L F L N M A D I O O A M E L
B U R M E E T L R N B E N S A
E N O I W H L O F R M O I I D
E F D G R U S R N H O W P W R
R M O B L I B C O G T Y P M I
T H E O D E N R J N U N I A E
T R I M O R O B I O D E P S L
```

Aragorn   Eowyn   Grima / Wormtongue   Saruman

Arwen   Faramir   Legolas   Sauron

Bilbo   Frodo   Merry   Shadowfax

Boromir   Galadriel   Nazgul   Shelob

Denethor   Gandalf   Pippin   Theoden

Elrond   Gimli   Quickbeam   Tom Bombadil

Eomer   Gollum   Samwise   Treebeard

125

This is an anagram crossword—unjumble the clue words and fit them into the corresponding places in the grid. Be careful though—some of these might have more than one potential answer…

Across

6. Snow

7. Canoes

8. Search

9. Isle

10. Petal

12. Rated

15. Redo

17. Bleats

19. Pineal

20. Soda

Down

1. Rosace

2. Chin

3. Ascot

4. Dermal

5. Neat

11. Picote

13. Posted

14. Bella

16. Lego

18. Deal

126

The names of six units of weight have been jumbled up below. Can you unscramble them and put their names back into the correct boxes?

A C ~~D D~~ D E E E ~~G~~ G ~~H~~ H I I K L M
~~N N~~ N N N O O O O O P R R S ~~T~~ T T ~~U~~ U U W

127

1. Restlessness, lack of sleep
2. Randomly
3. Tuitional, didactic
4. Silently
5. Only city in Canada's Northwest Territories
6. Destroyed completely
7. Very vivid shade of blue
8. Brilliantly, superbly
9. Deceptive, like a hallucination
10. On the spur of the moment
11. Duping, deceiving
12. Subtle; not noticeable or impositional
13. Meticulous, with great care
14. Things that must be done, responsibilities
15. Atheist
16. Defect of the shape of the eye
17. Setting for television's *The Simpsons*
18. Sport nicknamed ping-pong (5,6)
19. In a way that could be interpreted in different ways
20. Refreshed, made young or new again

#											
1		K		F							
2				Z							
3		U	C								
4			S				S		L		
5					K						
6	B										D
7				M							
8	O		D		F						
9									R	Y	
10	P										
11			D	W							
12			B		U						
13					K					G	
14			G								
15		N	B								
16			G							M	
17				F							
18									I		
19	M			U							
20			V					E			

128

A grid codeword puzzle. Given letters: 6 = W, 15 = O, 19 = F.

	2		19		21		26		5		21		6	
13	24	4	15		24	7	15	12	15	21	25	7	8	23
	26		2		5		14		11		5		25	
21	9	24	14	23	25		14	10	15	6 W	15 O	19 F	19	14
	13		8		7				23		19			
6	24	8	16	23	25	12	1		15	11	19	15	2	5
	12		24				9		1			24		
19	8	6	12		5	9	23	23	3		7	8	23	19
	4				15		7			15		25		
14	24	18	9	24	23		10	24	1	24	21	15	12	3
			12		5				15		17		18	
14	17	8	2	24	2	25	22		15	17	8	18	9	24
	9		24		9		9		1		5		25	
25	12	4	24	2	21	24	20	20	15		2	25	14	16
	16		23		14		20		23		24		10	

A B C D E F G H I J K L M N O P Q R S T U V W X Y Z

1	2	3	4	5	6	7	8	9	10	11	12	13
14	15	16	17	18	19	20	21	22	23	24	25	26

This is a game of dominoes! All the answers to the 24 clues have six letters, and fit into the grid in each set of six squares, beginning in each corresponding numbered square.

Answers can be written EITHER clockwise OR anticlockwise—you need to work that out! But just like dominoes, adjoining squares must share the same letter. So the answer to the first clue, MINUTE, has added some letters into the neighboring squares... Good luck!

1. Extremely small
2. Internal
3. Disappointment
4. Biblical hero, known for his strength
5. Electrical output
6. Private witticism or prank (2,4)
7. Verbiage, terminology
8. Approves; harmonizes
9. Continue again
10. Logo
11. Exchange a coupon
12. Contemporary
13. Mid-value average
14. Assisted
15. Breathe in
16. Vast Canadian bay
17. Legendary sailor
18. Himalayan nation
19. Try your hand at
20. Multiply by 2
21. Compensated for sin
22. Disguised
23. Degrade
24. Immune system organ

130

Here's a crossword that's a lot trickier than it looks. These are all one-word clues!

Across

7. Meek (6)

8. Certain (4-4)

9. Creative (8)

10. Nearby (6)

11. Killer (8)

12. Toward (6)

13. Hostile (11)

18. Donating (6)

20. Accompanied (8)

22. Injury (6)

23. Shoulder-blades (8)

24. Superb (8)

25. Oily (6)

Down

1. Dawn (7)

2. Constrain (8)

3. Deepnesses (6)

4. Break (8)

5. Exertion (6)

6. Intoxicated (7)

8. Anticipated (6-7)

14. Slowpokes (8)

15. Raised (8)

16. Disturb (7)

17. For (7)

19. Conditioned (6)

21. Bill (6)

131

Lots of overlaps in this wordsearch—all the answers contain at least three letters Ss!

```
N  P  E  O  O  A  S  S  E  N  G  U  M  S  N
I  S  P  P  E  C  N  S  K  C  A  S  S  O  C
L  T  A  S  P  O  T  S  S  U  B  N  S  S  E
O  W  S  B  S  A  S  S  I  S  T  E  D  S  M
S  N  S  T  N  S  M  A  S  C  T  E  P  E  I
S  S  E  T  C  S  S  E  N  I  S  O  N  N  S
A  T  S  K  H  B  N  R  S  S  U  S  K  T  T
S  E  O  I  I  E  R  E  S  S  A  S  S  R  R
S  P  N  S  S  A  F  R  E  A  E  I  U  U  E
E  S  T  U  S  Y  T  S  L  L  I  S  S  J  S
G  O  B  S  S  S  P  G  T  C  F  S  U  T  S
S  N  E  S  E  B  Y  H  F  P  I  A  R  P  C
H  S  O  S  T  P  S  A  U  S  S  U  R  E  D
S  T  S  I  S  N  O  C  N  S  S  Q  U  S  J
I  M  P  A  S  S  E  S  K  C  O  S  S  A  H
```

Asbestos	Consists	Justness	Quassias	Spyglass
Assisted	Cossacks	Messes up	Reassess	Stepsons
Business	Desserts	Mistress	Sassolin	Stetsons
Bus stops	Espouses	Nosiness	Saussure	
Chess set	Hassocks	Ossifies	Sisyphus	Stressed
Classics	Impasses	Passes on	Smugness	Susurrus

ⓘ DID YOU KNOW?

Before its dangers were full appreciated, asbestos was a wonder material. According to legend, the great king Charlemagne had a tablecloth spun from pure asbestos!

132

1. I think, therefore I _____ (2)

2. Ruin, spoil (3)

3. 500 sheets of paper (4)

4. Outer support of a painting (5)

5. Agricultural worker (6)

6. Between the wrist and the elbow (7)

7. Redesign or restyle a document (8)

8. Prepare a surface for living; make a planet more Earth-like (9)

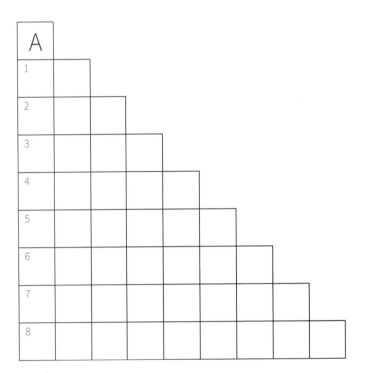

133

A   N

B   O

C   P

D   Q

E   R

F   S

G   T

H   U

I   V

J   W

K   X

L   Y

M   Z

1	11	21
2	12	22
3	13	23
4	14	24
5	15	25
6	16	26
7	17	
8	18	
9	19	
10	20	

134

1. Assessed the value of an antique

2. Stuttered, misspoken

3. Souvenirs

4. Having keen vision, like a bird (5-4)

5. An actor's fame or attention

6. Available only to a select few

7. Shaking nervously

8. Evidently, very clearly

9. Annoyances

10. Meaning, idea

11. Worse behaved

12. Thus

13. Stopped or paused momentarily

14. With vim

15. Woodworker

16. Word for word

17. Endured longer than

18. A numerical fact

19. Imagines

20. In a way that spares someone's feelings

#								
1	P				I			
2			M					
3	E					K		
4		G						
5				L		G		
6	X						V	
7			M	B				
8	B							Y
9		I				C		
10	N			N				N
11		U		H				
12					F			
13			I			T		
14		E						C
15			P					
16	I					L		
17	U		L					
18	T							C
19		V				G		
20		C		F				

5	26	2	9	14	22	9	25		21	18	2	2	9	22
26		1		24		1		13		1		14		6
8	24	12	23	12		21	24	6	1	25	17	24	26	3
12		10		2		24		17		9		26		16
24	9	2	26	2	22	6	1	22		24	18	11	5	6
11		22		10		19		12		17				19
	4	12	14	12	2	9		17	6	24	12	13	9	9
17		24		24						26		6		1
16	18	11	26	25	12	24		4	26	19	26	1	21	
23				17		12		6		26		25		6
2	1	6	8	18		14	26	19	26	13	10	6	24	2
26		13		20		12		9		9		21		14
7	18	26	20	20	26	14	6	13		21	9	9	2	9
18		15		13		12		26		9		1		1
9	13	9	19	9	1		18	1	9	25	26	22	9	25

A B C D E F G H I J K L M N O P Q R S T U V W X Y Z

1	2	3	4	5	6	7	8	9	10	11	12	13
14	15	16	17	18	19	20	21	22	23	24	25	26

136

What word is this?

__ __ LF - HE __ __ __ __ __

137

Across

6. Opinion (4)

7. High-pitched call (6)

8. Part of the eye (6)

9. Slope (4)

10. Silly, ridiculous (5)

12. Many-headed monster (5)

15. Large brass instrument (4)

17. Warm again (6)

19. Uproar, pandemonium (6)

20. Patient, long-suffering (4)

Down

1. Two-pointed hat (6)

2. Graceful waterbird (4)

3. Test the quality of metal (5)

4. A predator's prey (6)

5. Salve (4)

11. Tidily (6)

13. Wandered far and wide (6)

14. Painful muscular contraction (5)

16. Manipulated (4)

18. Rounded mass of earth (4)

138

Here's another wordsearch with a difference...

The clue words below aren't actually in the grid to be found—instead, two other words that can be made by rearranging their letters are hidden in the wordsearch on the left.

Solve the anagrams, then find the 14 rearranged words in the grid below!

F	S	P	A	L	T	R	Y	Y
I	D	S	A	I	L	E	D	L
E	E	E	L	O	S	K	O	T
L	T	G	K	A	T	R	M	R
F	A	I	T	S	E	L	F	A
I	K	R	E	D	A	D	D	P
T	S	D	I	J	L	T	I	R
S	U	L	D	U	S	T	E	R
R	G	E	S	E	T	A	L	S

Filets

_____

_____

Gilder

_____

_____

Ladies

_____

_____

Raptly

_____

_____

Rusted

_____

_____

Staked

_____

_____

Tassle

_____

_____

139

The answers to these questions can all be deduced correctly once you've worked out the connection between them...

1. What international aid organization is based in Geneva, Switzerland?
2. What British supermodel was the subject of a £1.5 million solid gold statue unveiled at the British Museum in 2008?
3. What does the medical abbreviation STML denote?
4. What classic novel of 1860 features the characters Tom and Maggie Tulliver?
5. Who was the lead singer of the Supremes?
6. What London train station was opened in 1852?
7. What is the common name for the constellation Crux?
8. What is the connection here?

140

Here's a general knowledge crossword to test your gray matter…

Across

8. Capital of Greece (6)

9. Earl Grey, e.g. (3)

10. Brother of Abel (4)

11. In business, SCM is supply chain ____ (10)

12. NBC show, *Law & Order: Special Victims* ____ (4)

13. To take in or soak up liquid (6)

16. Small toasted bread pieces served in soup (8)

17. Substance that induces an immune response in the body (7)

18. Bodily organ that has a fundus and pylorus (7)

22. A bodily pathway of energy in acupuncture (8)

25. Name shared by a late-night flight and a species of piranha (6)

26. Civil rights figure Ms. Parks (4)

27. BLTs and hoagies, for example (10)

30. Clara Bow was the original It ____ (4)

31. What the field of jurisprudence is concerned with (3)

32. Renowned scientific journal, founded 1869 (6)

Down

1. Italian volcano in eastern Sicily (4)

2. Spanish for "table" (4)

3. *Avengers* ____, Marvel comic book series (8)

4. Elastic toy, Mr. Armstrong (7)

5. Ruler of Cuba, died 2016 (6)

6. Used to (10)

7. Bodily sense controlled by the eyes (6)

14. It precedes appetit, marché, and voyage (3)

15. Initially, formerly (10)

19. Javelin, shot, and discus are the Olympic ____ events (8)

20. What an illachrymable person cannot do (3)

21. Tomb of the ____ Soldier, monument at Arlington (7)

23. Joe, Netflix's *Tiger King* (6)

24. Reflex form of the pronoun it (6)

28. Musical that features the song "Memory" (4)

29. Irish name for Ireland (4)

141

Here's a real challenge for you wordsearchers—the names of no less than 52 different five-letter animals are all hidden in this grid!

```
F O S S A P O N G O E S O O M
O K A A M A S K E W P L R T S
T Y I B D I R T A P I R O A P
T L G L L D O E P P U Z R H A
O L A E H H A T E B I Z A O D
P I F I S G L X N T K I N R E
I F N G R U N U O S S B G S D
O N O O S U O A G S W I N E I
Y F D D Y T M I T U R S O N N
W U I R A C O R T K B O O G N
T H A T I P O A R L I G E R H
A T E V C L S Y T O N I K A T
O U E L S H E E P I H I P P O
H T Y P P U P U D U A M A L L
S K U N K G U E J O C K O U S
```

Addax	Fitch	Kiang	Oribi	Shote	Takin
Burro	Fossa	Liger	Otary	Skunk	Tapir
Civet	Hinny	Llama	Pongo	Sloth	Tatou
Coypu	Hippo	Loris	Potto	Spade	Tigon
Dhole	Horse	Mhorr	Puppy	Spado	Urial
Dingo	Indri	Moose	Sable	Steer	Urson
Dogie	Izard	Mouse	Saiga	Stoat	Whelp
Felis	Jocko	Okapi	Sheep	Swine	Zibet
Filly	Kaama	Orang	Shoat		

142

Here's a fiendish extended version of one of the usual pyramid games. Each answer still contains all the letters of the previous one jumbled around—but once you reach a seven-letter answer here, you'll have to start taking one letter away to solve the next answer, and so on, until you're back down to one letter. Then, the answers start building up again, one letter at a time!

1. First name of actors Norton and Asner (2)

2. Female deer (3)

3. Elected leader of an Italian city state (4)

4. Present a complaint (5)

5. Glistening yellow (6)

6. Northern most county of Ireland (7)

7. Hang down loosely (6)

8. Famous Greek-Roman physician, died 216 CE (5)

9. Incline (4)

10. Beer (3)

11. Spanish masculine article (2)

12. French feminine article (2)

13. Deposit eggs (3)

14. Kill (4)

15. Briny (5)

16. Lopsided (6)

17. Bitterly, unpleasantly (7)

18. Level-headedness (6)

19. Devout person (5)

20. Sociable insects (4)

21. Positioned (3)

22. Because (2)

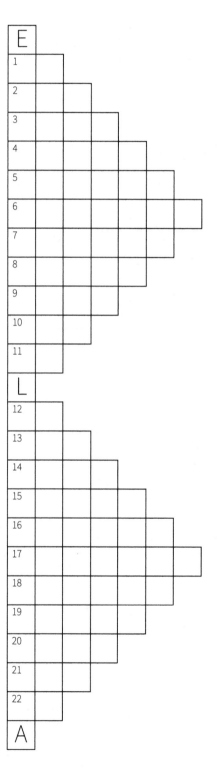

143

This is a double acrostic, so there are two extra hidden answers, reading down the shaded columns at the beginning and end of each line.

1. Having mixed or muted feelings; uncertain
2. Biblical peak (5,5)
3. Term formed from the first letters of others
4. Astutely experienced
5. A mixed salad platter; a random mixture
6. Recognizes correctly
7. Sacred; not to be touched or meddled with
8. Achieve
9. Encouraging
10. Decorating with ribbons
11. Remain somewhere during the colder months
12. Too busy or productive; hyper
13. Alcoholism
14. A youth
15. Transparent
16. Cut short, so as to produce a CLUE 3
17. West African nation
18. Unreasonable, unfounded
19. Real, genuine
20. 34th US president

ⓘ DID YOU KNOW?

The biblical mountain in CLUE 2 is in modern-day Egypt. Unusually, it is encircled by a series of secondary peaks, all of which are taller than it!

#								
1		M			V			
2		O			S			
3			I		I			
4		T				W		
5			M			U		
6		D				F		
7			C					C
8		C		O				
9			P	P				
10			R	L				N
11				R	W			
12		V						V
13			P			M		
14		D					C	
15			E		H			
16		B						
17			U					
18		R						A
19			G				M	
20								E

10	■	5	■	17	■	8	■	10	■	12	■	10	■	13
21	22	23	2	8	■	6	11	23	14	13	2	8	3	10
3	■	24	■	18	■	6	■	3	■	22	■	24	■	23
3	4	11	5	22	16	15	■	8	18	4	26	11	2	2
■	■	14	■	■	■	■	■	22	■	■	14	■	11	
21	9	21	8	14	■	25	21	13	■	3	23	25	■	5
26	■	■	■	23	■	23	■	2	■	20	■	13	■	■
2	13	22	■	22	13	19	8	25	21	23	■	1	15	7
■	■	2	■	13	■	1	■	21	■	13	■	■	■	21
3	■	13	26	2	■	2	21	24	■	25	11	13	23	24
20	■	3	■	■	■	13	■	■	■	■	■	25	■	■
23	7	3	5	13	8	19	■	16	21	21	14	2	23	10
13	■	13	■	22	■	8	■	23	■	23	■	13	■	8
26	15	22	16	16	13	17	11	2	■	22	21	17	11	18
4	■	5	■	15	■	11	■	4	■	16	■	11	■	24

A B C D E F G H I J K L M N O P Q R S T U V W X Y Z

1	2	3	4	5	6	7	8	9	10	11	12	13

14	15	16	17	18	19	20	21	22	23	24	25	26

145

Ten Summer Olympics host cities have been jumbled together below and their letters placed in alphabetical order. Can you unjumble their names and place them into the correct boxes?

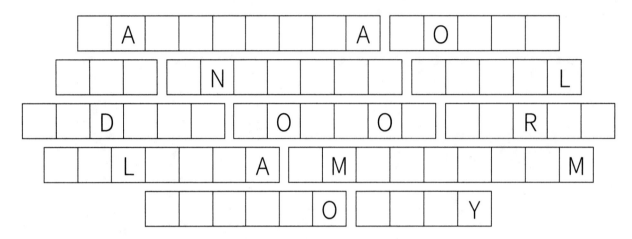

A A A A A A A A A B C C C D D D E E E E E E G I I I K L L L L L L M M M N N N N N N O O O O O O O O P R R R S S S S S S T T T T T U X Y Y Y Y

146

1. Symbol found in all email address

2. Prepare leather

3. Against

4. Silk-like fabric

5. Legendary offspring of Uranus and Gaia

6. Put in place or position

7. Most sharp-tasting

8. Saying again

9. Smashing

10. Puts in order; makes flat or uncurled

11. They're "tugged" by melancholic stories

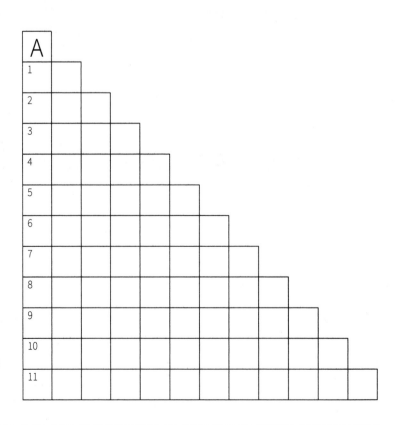

147

Arrange the six-letter blocks on the right into the correct places in the grid on the left to spell out the names of 12 six-letter European cities, one on each row.

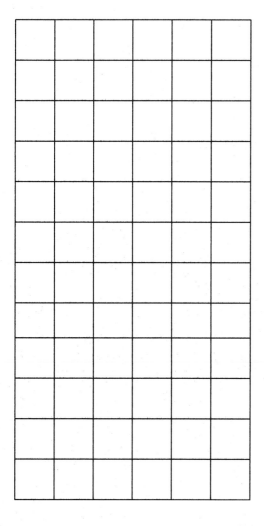

G	R
N	D
A	
N	

L	O
K	R
	U
	I

N	
N	
A	T
Z	A

	R
	L
A	N	T
A	

I	D
I	N
	S
	S

N	N	A
G		E
		N

M	
V		F
P	R	A

		E
P	L	E
H	E	

N	S
E	B
O	N

M	A	D
D	U	B

K	O	W
I	C	H

		U
L	I	S	B	O

148

Which presidents had these as their middle names?

1. Jefferson

2. Knox

3. Robinette

4. Milhous

5. Gamamliel

6. Alan

149

What word is this?

__ __ __ GR __ __ U __ A __ E

150

A final set of tricky questions…all linked by the same initials.

1. What name is Batman's sidekick Robin also known?

2. How might you also describe a twitcher, or an ornithologist?

3. What is a dish of fillet steak wrapped and cooked in pastry known as?

4. What conflicts took place between 1880–1, and 1899–1902?

5. Who had a 1974 hit with "You're the First, the Last, My Everything"?

6. How is the venomous creature Latrodectus more commonly known?

7. What Hollywood actor was born in Idar-Oberstein, Germany, in 1955?

8. What Arctic creature is nicknamed the melonhead, or the sea canary?

SOLUTIONS

1

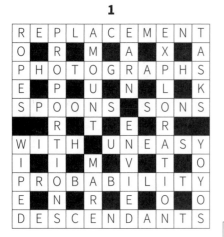

4

9

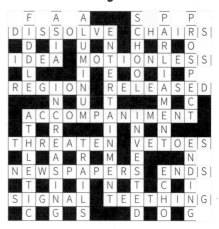

5

1. Milwaukee 2. McCartney
3. Monopoly 4. Moustaches
5. Matthew 6. Mary 7. Montana
8. The Mavericks 9. Misery 10. Martha
11. Manatee 12. Mexico 13. Muslim
14. Mae West 15. Mamma Mia!
16. Mediterranean 17. Mr. Magoo
18. Mercedes 19. Magic 20. Moby-Dick

6

SPRINGTIME

10

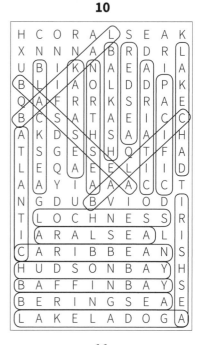

2

Hidden phrase: David Bowie

3

D	E	C	E	M	B	E	R
A	L	P	H	A	B	E	T
V	E	R	T	I	C	A	L
I	C	E	C	R	E	A	M
D	U	T	C	H	M	A	N
B	I	G	A	P	P	L	E
O	P	T	I	M	I	S	T
W	H	I	S	T	L	E	R
I	N	S	U	L	T	E	D
E	V	I	D	E	N	C	E

7

S						
A	S					
S	E	A				
S	E	A	R			
E	R	A	S	E		
E	A	S	T	E	R	
A	U	S	T	E	R	E
T	R	E	A	S	U	R	E
C	R	E	A	T	U	R	E	S

8

QUEBEC,
ALBERTA,
SASKATCHEWAN

11

12

A						
P	A					
A	S	P				
P	A	I	N			
S	P	A	I	N		
S	P	R	A	I	N	
P	E	R	S	I	A	N
P	A	I	N	T	E	R	S
T	E	R	R	A	P	I	N	S

13

Hidden phrase: Maintain the status quo

16

1. Japan 2. Drum 3. REM 4. Zsa-Zsa
5. Knee 6. Lions 7. Pewter
8. Washington 9. Skyscraper
10. Mutton 11. Venison 12. Inches
13. *The Hobbit* 14. Canada
15. February 16. Niçoise 17. Quakers
18. Barcelona 19. Grieg 20. Uganda
21. Eight 22. X-Men
23. Antepen ultimate 24. YouTube
25. Times Square 26. *Oliver!*

17

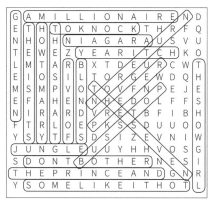

21

22

Hidden phrase:
When push comes to shove

14

15

18

19

20

BOOKCASE

23

24

FOOLPROOF

25

HITCHCOCK,
SPIELBERG,
TARANTINO

26

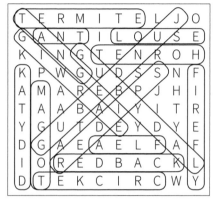

Anagram answers: Katydid, Earwig,
Ladybug, Redback, Termite, Flea,
Firefly, Louse, Spider, Cricket, Ant,
Gnat, Hornet, Maggot

27

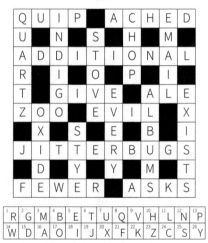

28

1. The Owl and the Pussycat
2. The Eagles 3. *The Maltese Falcon*
4. Cardinal 5. Blue Jays
6. Chickenpox 7. *Swan Lake*
8. *Goosebumps* 9. Robin Williams
10. All the answers contain the
names of birds: Owl, Eagle, Falcon,
Cardinal, Blue Jay, Chicken,
Swan, Goose, Robin

29

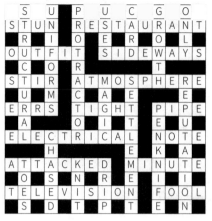

30

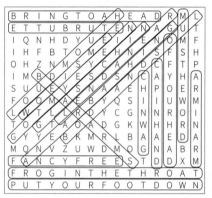

31

S	C	R	E	W
A		U		A
F	I	R	E	D
E		A		E
R	U	L	E	D

32

A							
G	A						
R	A	G					
R	A	G	E				
G	R	A	D	E			
B	A	D	G	E	R		
A	B	R	I	D	G	E	
B	R	I	G	A	D	E	S
B	I	R	D	C	A	G	E	S

33

I	C	E	H	O	C	K	E	Y
N	A	N	T	U	C	K	E	T
D	A	L	M	A	T	I	A	N
U	N	B	U	C	K	L	E	D
S	O	M	E	T	I	M	E	S
T	H	E	R	E	F	O	R	E
R	E	T	R	A	I	N	E	D
I	N	T	E	L	L	E	C	T
A	D	J	E	C	T	I	V	E
L	O	C	A	T	I	O	N	S
R	E	S	P	O	N	D	E	D
E	V	E	R	Y	B	O	D	Y
V	I	R	T	U	A	L	L	Y
O	P	E	R	A	T	I	O	N
L	O	O	P	H	O	L	E	S
U	N	C	H	A	N	G	E	D
T	I	M	E	Z	O	N	E	S
I	N	T	E	R	R	U	P	T
O	I	N	T	M	E	N	T	S
N	O	C	T	U	R	N	A	L

Hidden phrase: Industrial revolution

34

35

PROFESSIONAL

36

37

F	I	G	H	T	E	R
A	R	T	I	S	A	N
R	E	S	U	M	E	D
A	N	Y	T	I	M	E
N	E	E	D	I	N	G
D	I	S	A	B	L	E
A	C	R	O	B	A	T
W	A	R	B	L	E	R
A	N	N	O	Y	E	D
Y	I	E	L	D	E	D

Hidden phrase: Far and away

38

1. *Top Gun* 2. Tear gland
3. The Grenadines 4. *The Godfather*
5. Tail-gating 6. Terry Gilliam
7. The Gap 8. *True Grit*
9. Thomas Gray 10. The Gambia
11. Greater than 12. George Takei
13. Globetrotters 14. Guten Tag
15. Ghost town 16. Globe Theatre
17. *Good Times* 18. Golf tee
19. *Gulliver's Travels* 20. Gene Tierney

39

40

41

42

| H |
S	H
A	S	H
D	A	S	H
S	H	A	D	E
S	H	A	R	E	D
H	A	R	D	E	S	T
H	E	A	D	R	E	S	T
S	H	A	T	T	E	R	E	D

43

H	A	L	L	O	W	E	E	N
O	F	F	E	N	S	I	V	E
L	I	G	H	T	N	I	N	G
L	I	M	I	T	L	E	S	S
Y	E	S	T	E	R	D	A	Y
W	I	N	D	O	W	B	O	X
O	T	H	E	R	W	I	S	E
O	U	T	E	R	M	O	S	T
D	I	G	E	S	T	I	O	N
B	A	C	H	E	L	O	R	S
L	I	G	H	T	Y	E	A	R
O	R	N	A	M	E	N	T	S
C	A	R	D	B	O	A	R	D
K	N	O	W	L	E	D	G	E
B	A	S	I	C	A	L	L	Y
U	N	D	E	R	W	E	A	R
S	T	R	A	N	G	E	S	T
T	E	M	P	O	R	A	R	Y
E	S	C	A	L	A	T	O	R
R	E	C	T	A	N	G	L	E

Hidden phrase:
Hollywood blockbuster

44

45

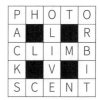

46

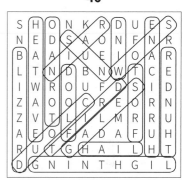

47

48

1. "Deck the Halls" 2. *King Kong*
3. Fighter ace, flying ace 4. Queensland
5. Shuffleboard 6. *Suits* 7. Diamond
8. Jack Palance 9. Heart 10. All the
answers have something to do with
playing cards: Deck, King, Ace, Queen,
Shuffle, Suit, Diamond, Jack, Heart

49

		T	H		C			D	C	
T	O	R	N	A	D	O		P	R	O	P	O	S	E
I		I	W		O			O	C	N				A
C	O	M	M	A		P	E	R	S	U	A	D	E	S
K			I		E			K	M	I				I
L	U	C	K	I	E	R		B	E	A	T	E	N	
E		O		A		A		N		I				G
	I	N	V	E	S	T	I	G	A	T	I	O	N	
I		S	X		E		R		N					C
C	H	O	P	P	Y			E	M	B	A	S	S	Y
I		N		O		P		E		E				C
C	L	A	S	S	R	O	O	M		A	W	F	U	L
L		N		I		R		E		S		A		E
E	X	T	I	N	C	T		N	O	T	I	C	E	D
		S		G				T		S		E		

50

51

(crossword grid)

52

F	A	M	O	U	S
R	A	B	B	I	T
A	L	L	O	W	S
N	E	E	D	E	D
K	N	O	C	K	S
E	U	R	O	P	E
N	I	B	B	L	E
S	A	L	A	D	S
T	H	E	O	R	Y
E	A	T	I	N	G
I	N	L	A	W	S
N	O	D	D	E	D
S	T	R	U	C	K
M	I	D	D	L	E
O	C	E	A	N	S
N	O	Z	Z	L	E
S	O	B	B	E	D
T	I	P	T	O	E
E	X	H	A	L	E
R	E	V	E	R	T

Hidden phrase: Frankenstein's monster

53

1 K	2 H	3 B	4 S	5 X	6 N	7 E	8 L	9 F	10 M	11 C	12 R	13 W
14 T	15 V	16 J	17 D	18 P	19 O	20 A	21 Q	22 Z	23 I	24 Y	25 G	26 U

54

D	R	A	M	A
E		L		W
S	T	I	F	F
K		K		U
S	P	E	L	L

55

N							
U	N						
N	U	T					
U	N	T	O				
C	O	U	N	T			
T	O	U	C	A	N		
A	U	C	T	I	O	N	
C	A	U	T	I	O	N	S
T	E	N	A	C	I	O	U	S

56

1. Shuttlecock 2. Plymouth Rock
3. Patrick 4. Silverback 5. Ayers Rock
6. Gregory Peck 7. Hockey stick
8. Donald Duck 9. Sandra Bullock
10. John Steinbeck 11. The Dome of
the Rock 12. New Brunswick
13. Woodstock 14. Limerick
15. Innsbruck 16. Gatwick
17. *Moonstruck* 18. Benjamin Spock
19. Jackson Pollock 20. Forelock

57

(crossword grid)

58

59

R	E	A	L	I	S	M
E	A	R	N	I	N	G
S	C	R	E	E	C	H
H	O	S	T	I	L	E
U	N	E	A	R	T	H
F	L	O	W	E	R	S
F	A	I	N	T	E	D
L	O	C	A	T	E	S
E	N	T	A	I	L	S
D	O	U	B	L	E	S

Hidden phrase: Reshuffled

60

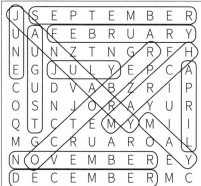

61

A	B	D	I	C	A	T	E
L	A	B	R	A	D	O	R
L	I	F	E	L	I	K	E
S	A	B	O	T	E	U	R
W	O	O	D	L	A	N	D
E	D	U	C	A	T	E	D
L	E	V	I	T	A	T	E
L	A	B	O	R	D	A	Y
T	I	M	E	O	U	T	S
H	E	D	G	E	H	O	G
A	L	C	A	P	O	N	E
T	O	B	O	G	G	A	N
E	N	C	I	R	C	L	E
N	U	M	B	E	R	E	D
D	I	L	E	M	M	A	S
S	O	R	C	E	R	E	R
W	H	I	T	E	O	U	T
E	N	T	A	N	G	L	E
L	E	T	H	A	R	G	Y
L	A	U	N	C	H	E	D

Hidden phrase:
All's well that ends well

62

63

B	R	A	S	I	L	I	A
E	G	G	P	L	A	N	T
W	I	S	T	E	R	I	A
A	P	P	R	O	V	E	S
R	E	I	N	V	E	S	T
E	N	V	E	L	O	P	E
T	W	O	B	Y	T	W	O
H	I	T	I	T	O	F	F
E	Y	E	S	I	G	H	T
I	N	A	F	L	A	S	H
D	A	I	Q	U	I	R	I
E	L	E	C	T	I	O	N
S	P	E	A	K	I	N	G
O	B	S	C	U	R	E	S
F	O	R	E	C	A	S	T
M	O	S	Q	U	I	T	O
A	T	H	L	E	T	I	C
R	I	O	B	R	A	V	O
C	H	R	O	M	I	U	M
H	A	N	D	S	O	M	E

Hidden phrases: Beware the ides of
March; A taste of things to come

64

1. Aardvark, aardwolf 2. Mediterranean
Avenue, Boardwalk 3. "I Want To Hold
Your Hand", "She Loves You"
4. Swan, crane 5. North Sea, Irish Sea 6.
To Catch a Thief, North by Northwest 7.
Love, deuce 8. Pawn, king 9. i and
j—the tittle is the dot! 10. Oregon,
Arizona 11. *A Tale of Two Cities, Pride
and Prejudice* 12. John Tyler, Millard
Fillmore 13. C, M 14. France, Finland
15. Anne Boleyn, Anne of Cleves

65

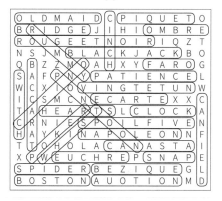

66

67

68

ORGAN, HARPSICHORD, PIANO,
HARMONIUM, ACCORDION

69

RESPONSIBILITY

70

CACTUS
ELBOWS
NEATER
TALKED
RAZORS
ABROAD
LARGER
NARROW
EIGHTY
REFUSE
VENDOR
ONEILL
UNISON
STRIVE
SIPPED
YAWNED
SNOOZE
TRIVIA
EIFFEL
MIDDAY

Hidden phrase:
Central nervous system

73

JASPER, RUBY, DIAMOND, JADE,
SAPPHIRE, GARNET, ONYX, AMETHYST,
AQUAMARINE, OPAL, TOPAZ, PERIDOT

74

S T E E R
A ■ N ■ I
V O T E S
E ■ E ■ E
D A R E S

75

1. Armenia 2. Alan Alda 3. Arena
4. Alaska 5. Athena 6. Angina
7. Arachnophobia 8. *A Passage to India*
9. Antigua and Barbuda
10. *Antony and Cleopatra*
11. A cappella 12. Adriatic Sea
13. Alexandria 14. Anaconda
15. Anthony Minghella

78

R
R A
E A R
L E A R
E A R L S
A L E R T S
A N T L E R S
L A T R I N E S
G N A R L I E S T

79

CAPPUCCINO, LATTE, AMERICANO,
ESPRESSO, CORTADO

80

ANIMATORS
PRUDISHLY
PORTENDED
APPOINTEE
LEDASTRAY
AFTERWARD
CRABBIEST
HOMEGROWN
INHERITED
ADAMANTLY
NEWCASTLE
MERCILESS
OMNIVORES
UNDERDONE
NUMBSKULL
TOLERATES
AMBUSHING
ILLOGICAL
NAMECHECK
SHRUBBERY

71

1	2	3	4	5	6	7	8	9	10	11	12	13
J	U	Z	Y	K	E	V	A	Q	S	X	N	R

14	15	16	17	18	19	20	21	22	23	24	25	26
W	O	B	F	D	M	C	L	H	T	I	P	G

72

I
I P
P I E
R I P E
P E T R I
P I R A T E
T R A I P S E
P A R A S I T E
D I S P A R A T E

76

77

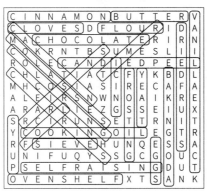

81

1	2	3	4	5	6	7	8	9	10	11	12	13
K	M	Z	U	H	B	E	T	Q	V	S	W	A

14	15	16	17	18	19	20	21	22	23	24	25	26
I	N	F	J	G	R	X	L	O	P	C	Y	D

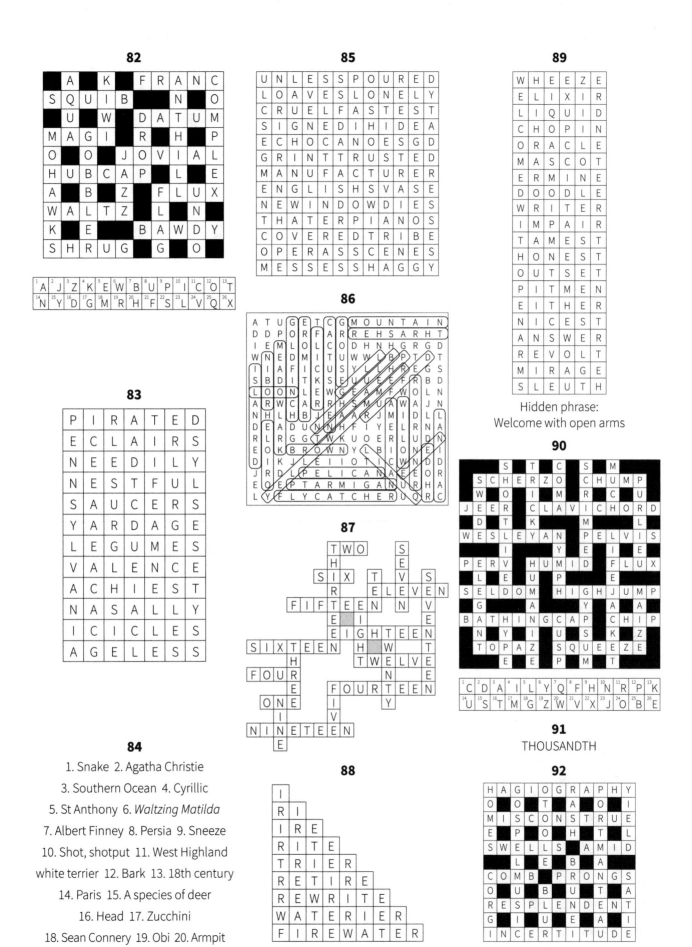

82

85

89

86

83

87

90

Hidden phrase:
Welcome with open arms

91
THOUSANDTH

84

1. Snake 2. Agatha Christie
3. Southern Ocean 4. Cyrillic
5. St Anthony 6. *Waltzing Matilda*
7. Albert Finney 8. Persia 9. Sneeze
10. Shot, shotput 11. West Highland
white terrier 12. Bark 13. 18th century
14. Paris 15. A species of deer
16. Head 17. Zucchini
18. Sean Connery 19. Obi 20. Armpit

88

92

93

BLIZZARD, SNOWDRIFT, WHITEOUT, ICE, AVALANCHE

94

1. Mausoleum 2. Madison Square Garden 3. Artemis 4. Pyramid 5. Olympia 6. *The Colossus* 7. Lighthouse 8. The Seven Wonders of the World: the Mausoleum at Halicarnassus; the Hanging Gardens of Babylon; the Temple of Artemis; the Great Pyramid of Giza; the Statue of Zeus at Olympia; the Colossus of Rhodes; the Lighthouse of Alexandria.

95

I	N	D	I	G	O
P	U	R	P	L	E
O	R	A	N	G	E
M	A	R	O	O	N
Y	E	L	L	O	W
C	E	R	I	S	E
B	R	O	N	Z	E
S	I	L	V	E	R
V	I	O	L	E	T
B	L	O	N	D	E

96

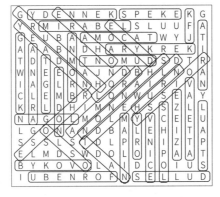

97

98

99

T	A	B	A	S	C	O
W	E	I	G	H	T	Y
O	P	I	N	I	N	G
B	E	G	U	I	L	E
I	M	P	I	N	G	E
R	E	D	A	C	T	S
D	A	B	B	I	N	G
S	A	M	P	L	E	D
W	H	I	T	T	L	E
I	N	V	A	L	I	D
T	I	G	H	T	E	N
H	E	P	A	T	I	C
O	N	S	T	A	G	E
N	E	T	T	L	E	S
E	D	I	T	O	R	S
S	M	O	O	T	H	S
T	I	P	P	L	E	S
O	S	P	R	E	Y	S
N	I	T	P	I	C	K
E	S	T	U	A	R	Y

Hidden phrase:
Two birds with one stone

100

101

102

CONJUGATE

103

1. Spanish 2. Red 3. Bear 4. Meander 5. Orchids 6. Femur 7. Lafayette 8. Charles 9. Zaire 10. Einstein 11. Whip 12. Argentina 13. Harold 14. Kim Kardashian 15. Neuralgia 16. Yugoslavia 17. Tina Turner 18. Paddington Bear 19. India 20. Xerox 21. David 22. Vermont 23. January 24. Uruguay 25. *Quantum Leap* 26. Gresham's Law

104

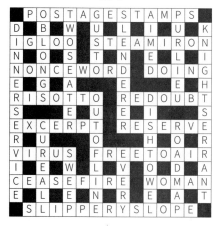

105

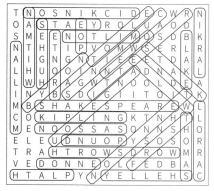

Hidden phrase: "Two roads diverged in a wood, and I— I took the one less traveled by" from Robert Frost's *The Road Not Taken*

106

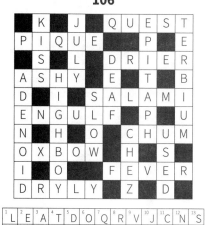

107

KOALA, WOMBAT, KANGAROO, TASMANIAN DEVIL, WALLABY, POSSUM

108

Hidden phrase: Hubble Space Telescope

109

R S H M F A E
WHIP P OVEREXPOSE E
A L R O E O P
OPTICS S WISEGUYS S
S T E E
DOZE PROVIDENCE E
D O X N O
PIED WHIFF JINX
Z E D L U S
DEEPFREEZE NEED
L X K Q
CATACOMB INFLUX
L C A U B O E
EGOISTICAL OINK
A D H K E D T

1	2	3	4	5	6	7	8	9	10	11	12	13
I	Q	R	K	S	L	V	O	C	P	N	U	B

14	15	16	17	18	19	20	21	22	23	24	25	26
D	J	X	M	H	G	Z	Y	F	W	E	A	T

110

Anagram answers: 2. MANICURE (+ E), 3. TERRAPIN (+A), 4. BLUNDER (+R), 5. PAWS (-S), 6. REPLICA (+I), 7. NIGHTLY (+G), 8. WRITES (-H), 9. SPATULA (+T), 10. ELEVEN (+E), 11. BOREDOM (+D), 12. DANDER (+N), 13. SCENIC (-E), 14. SKIING (+S), 15. TRIPLANE (-S) Hidden word: Nearsightedness

111

T
ET
ENT
TEEN
EATEN
NEGATE
ELEGANT
ENTANGLE
GENTLEMAN

112

1. Hammer 2. White 3. James Whale
4. Tiger 5. Sitting Bull 6. Goblins
7. *Nurse Jackie* 8. Lemon
9. Great Barrier Reef 10. Greenland
11. Salmon 12. Hammer(head), (great) white, whale, tiger, bull, goblin, nurse, lemon, reef, Greenland and salmon are all species of shark

113

LARDIEST
AILMENTS
TAILORED
IDOLATRY
NOMINATE
QUAINTER
UPSTREAM
ABSURDLY
RECITALS
TANGIBLE
ENTAILED
RAWHIDES

Hidden phrase: Latin Quarter

114

LAWNMOWER

115

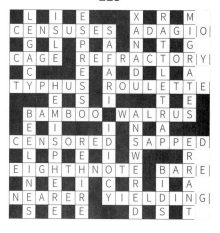

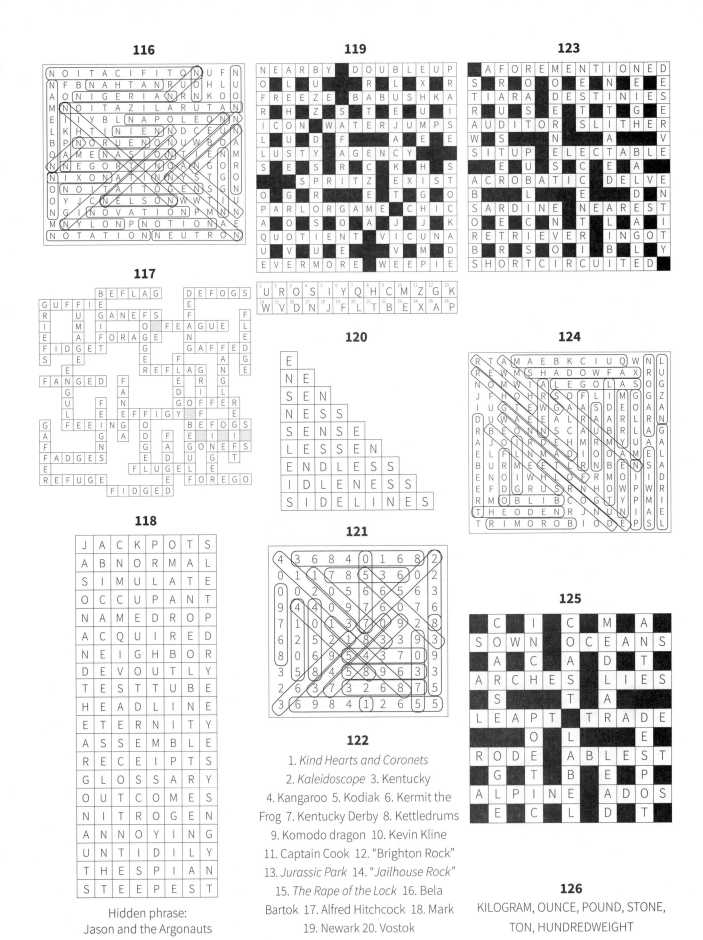

116

117

118

Hidden phrase:
Jason and the Argonauts

119

120

121

122

1. *Kind Hearts and Coronets*
2. *Kaleidoscope* 3. Kentucky
4. Kangaroo 5. Kodiak 6. Kermit the
Frog 7. Kentucky Derby 8. Kettledrums
9. Komodo dragon 10. Kevin Kline
11. Captain Cook 12. "Brighton Rock"
13. *Jurassic Park* 14. *"Jailhouse Rock"*
15. *The Rape of the Lock* 16. Bela
Bartok 17. Alfred Hitchcock 18. Mark
19. Newark 20. Vostok

123

124

125

126
KILOGRAM, OUNCE, POUND, STONE,
TON, HUNDREDWEIGHT

127

```
W A K E F U L N E S S
H A P H A Z A R D L Y
E D U C A T I O N A L
N O I S E L E S S L Y
Y E L L O W K N I F E
O B L I T E R A T E D
U L T R A M A R I N E
W O N D E R F U L L Y
I L L U S I O N A R Y
S P O N T A N E O U S
H O O D W I N K I N G
U N O B T R U S I V E
P A I N S T A K I N G
O B L I G A T I O N S
N O N B E L I E V E R
A S T I G M A T I S M
S P R I N G F I E L D
T A B L E T E N N I S
A M B I G U O U S L Y
R E J U V E N A T E D
```

Hidden phrase:
When you wish upon a star

130

131

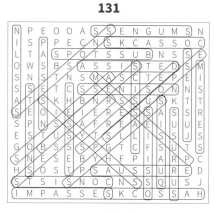

128

```
G R Y T D W C A U H X N V
14 15 16 17 18 19 20 21 22 23 24 25 26
S O K P Q F Z M B L E I J
```

132

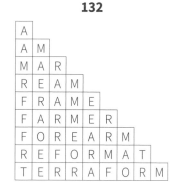

```
A
A M
M A R
R E A M
F R A M E
F A R M E R
F O R E A R M
R E F O R M A T
T E R R A F O R M
```

129

133

134

```
A P P R A I S E D
S T A M M E R E D
K E E P S A K E S
E A G L E E Y E D
L I M E L I G H T
E X C L U S I V E
T R E M B L I N G
O B V I O U S L Y
N U I S A N C E S
I N T E N T I O N
N A U G H T I E R
T H E R E F O R E
H E S I T A T E D
E N E R G E T I C
C A R P E N T E R
L I T E R A L L Y
O U T L A S T E D
S T A T I S T I C
E N V I S A G E S
T A C T F U L L Y
```

Hidden phrase:
A skeleton in the closet

135

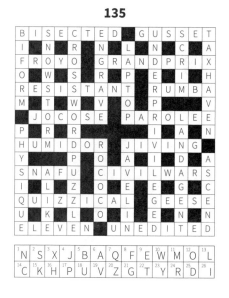

```
1 2 3 4 5 6 7 8 9 10 11 12 13
N S X J B A Q F E W M O L
14 15 16 17 18 19 20 21 22 23 24 25 26
C K H P U V Z G T Y R D I
```

136
HALF-HEARTED

137

138

Anagram answers: ITSELF, STIFLE;
GLIDER, GIRDLE; IDEALS, SAILED;
PARTLY, PALTRY; RUDEST, DUSTER;
SKATED, TASKED; STEALS, SLATES

139

1. The Red Cross 2. Kate Moss
3. Short-term memory loss
4. *The Mill on the Floss* 5. Diana Ross
6. King's Cross 7. Southern Cross
8. All the answers end in –OSS

140

141

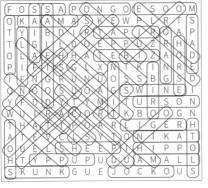

142

143

Hidden phrases: A miss is as good as a
mile; Time is the great healer

144

G	L	S	K	T	F	P	I	V	M	E	J	A
D	Y	H	Z	N	R	Q	O	C	U	X	B	W

145

BARCELONA, TOKYO, LOS ANGELES,
SEOUL, SYDNEY, LONDON, PARIS,
ATLANTA, AMSTERDAM, MEXICO CITY

146

147

148

1. Bill Clinton
2. James K Polk
3. Joe Biden
4. Richard Nixon
5. Warren G Harding
6. Chester A Arthur

149

CONGRATULATE

150

1. Boy wonder
2. Bird watcher
3. Beef wellington
4. Boer wars
5. Barry white
6. Black widow
7. Bruce willis
8. Beluga whale.